William Gilbert

The rosary

a legend of Wilton Abbey

William Gilbert

The rosary
a legend of Wilton Abbey

ISBN/EAN: 9783741191824

Manufactured in Europe, USA, Canada, Australia, Japa

Cover: Foto ©Andreas Hilbeck / pixelio.de

Manufactured and distributed by brebook publishing software (www.brebook.com)

William Gilbert

The rosary

THE ROSARY.

INTRODUCTION.

AMONG the various mischiefs arising from the dissolution of religious houses in the reign of Henry the Eighth, one, and not the least, was the loss to literature, occasioned by the dispersion of the records belonging to many of the more important of these institutions. Of these, perhaps the Benedictine convent at Wilton might be named among the saddest examples. It is melancholy to note how small a portion of the voluminous documents that once belonged to that wealthy convent is now in existence—how few instances of the pious lives and labours of its inmates can be quoted; even that of the very list of its abbesses is most incomplete. But in this case, as in many other instances where the malice of man has been exerted to hide the works and efforts of the godly, tradition has stepped forward, and from her records, more durable than graven brass, has brought forth a singular episode in the life of one of the convent inmates which would otherwise have been lost to the world.

The heroine of the following pages is a singular specimen of this extraordinary power of tradition. Although for many years abbess of the convent, her name does not even appear on any of the convent records or lists. Her very existence would have remained unknown had not chance revealed the fact of the present written confession in the library of a celebrated Wiltshire antiquarian; and he, as jealous of his ancient manuscripts as a sultan of his harem, now sighs over the escape of the present recital, and its exposure to the rude eyes of the world.

That she existed and was in her day one of the wealthiest and best beloved superiors the convent ever had, is certain; but from what family she originally sprang is exceedingly obscure. She appears to have succeeded Edith Barogh, of whom she was a distant relative; but as nothing more is known of that abbess than her name, and that she began her rule A.D. 1464, little can be obtained from that source—even the date of her death is uncertain. The name of our heroine was Alicia Longspée, widow of Edwin Longspée, a descendant of William, first Earl of Salisbury. She had been a widow several months before she entered the convent as a novice. As she was then young, exceedingly beautiful, and very wealthy, her retirement from the world caused great wonder to most; but to others who knew her during her married life, her quiet retiring disposition, intense love for her husband, as well as her great piety, the act was not so extraordinary. How many years she ruled over the convent is uncertain. Tradition reports her reign to have been strict yet gentle, and she was much loved, not only by those immediately under her control, but by both rich and poor for many miles round. She was succeeded by Alice Comalonde, of whose election there is also no date.

Alicia Longspée's death was occasioned by a disease of the lungs, arising from a severe cold. She had made a short pilgrimage to a shrine in Salisbury Cathedral, and on returning was caught in a violent storm, from which she was unable to obtain shelter. Finding her end approaching, and determining that her death should conduce to the cause of the holy Catholic Church, she requested permission of the Bishop of Salisbury to make a written confession, which might be kept sealed not only till after her death, but till the Christmas-eve following it, when it should be read to the nuns assembled in the refectory between vespers and the celebration of midnight mass. The bishop, after some demur, fearing scandal might possibly arise, at last gave his permission, and the confession was forthwith written out on parchment. Alicia shortly afterwards expired in the odour of sanctity, and was interred in the convent cemetery. A rosary she had always worn attached to her dress, was, at her request, buried with her. Her confession was kept sealed as she had desired, till the following Christmas-eve, when it was read to the assembled sisterhood.

CHAPTER I.

HAVING obtained permission from the Bishop of Salisbury to make a written confession of certain sins committed by me before I entered the holy house of which I have been ten years abbess, and considering that the open recital of my faults might be advantageous to our sisterhood, as proving the great power and goodness of God, and feeling that the strength of the mortal malady under which I am at present suffering will shortly relieve me from the cares and dangers of this life, I request that, on the evening preceding Christmas day, between vespers and the celebration of midnight mass, this confession may, for the following reasons, be read aloud to the sisterhood :—

1st. That the narration of the strong temptations to which I was exposed for two years prior to my seeking shelter within the convent walls, will, I believe, tend to the greater honour of God and our blessed Lady, who snatched me from the pit of perdition which yawned before me.

2d. It may shew how great is the mercy and power of God in assisting those in sore extremity who call upon Him for comfort and support.

And lastly, that by this candid avowal of my fault I may perform a work of humility acceptable to God, in shewing to those now dwelling in our house at present under my spiritual authority, and to others who have too often held me in higher estimation than was my due, that I have been a great and wicked sinner, and should have been totally unworthy

A Legend of Wilton Abbey. 5

to hold communion hereafter with the Blessed, had it not been for the great mercy of Heaven vouchsafed to me in my need.

I will commence the thread of my confession three years after my marriage with my dear husband, and two years before I took the veil. I will describe him as he appeared to me the last time I saw him—to do so as he appeared to me when I married him would be impossible.

He was tall, handsome, powerful, and brave. A nobler looking knight was not at the court, nor one whose appearance better told his high qualities. He was generous but not extravagant, learned but not pedantic, resolute as a lion yet gentle as a lamb. He was beautiful in countenance; his eyes beamed with an expression of love and gentleness seldom met with in men, while the whole expression of his face told of his noble, loving nature. I will not dwell longer on his appearance, for I find I cannot do him justice. I would not have attempted it, but it is necessary to describe in some sort his noble qualities and beauty to make the enormity of my fault appear in its proper light, and the bounty of Heaven in saving me from the horrible sin I might otherwise have been guilty of, appear the greater.

After we had been married nearly three years, when we were residing in perfect happiness at the castle in Berkshire, my husband received an order from the king to attend the court. At that time his majesty was residing in Crosby Palace. To obey with the utmost alacrity every command of his king was a paramount duty with my husband; and in two days after he had received the summons, he left the castle for London.

We had never before been parted, and it would be difficult for me to explain to you the great grief his absence occasioned me. I wandered by myself in the park, and wept as if I fancied the intensity of my sorrow would induce my husband to return and console me. I wandered through every room in the castle, but found all desolate from his absence, though all our people appeared to sympathise with me and do all in their power to cheer and console me.

The first night of his absence was to me one of continued sorrow. I slept not a moment, and in the morning my pillow was bathed with my tears. Next day my sorrow had not abated, and I passed another of lonely misery. The third appeared still longer than the others, for I began to hope some message might arrive from my lord to inform me of his safe arrival, little thinking it was nearly seventy miles to London, and to receive intelligence of him so soon was impossible. Another day passed, and another; but at last a messenger arrived from him with a letter.

My behaviour, when I understood the man came from my lord, was rather that of a demented woman than a retiring wife. I did not give him time to alight from his horse, but almost tore the letter from his hand. He must have been surprised at my rude behaviour, but I saw him not, my eyes so feasted on the letter, and I almost cried with rage that the cord that bound it was too strong for me to break with my hands. In vain did I try till the cord cut me like a knife. I almost screamed with anger at my servant girl that she did not bring me something to sever it with. At last a man-at-arms brought me his poignard. I took it from his hand, and was on the point of cutting the cord when I thought it was an ill omen that a dagger should cut the cord that bound my lord's letter, and I gave it back again. At last Bertha, my waiting-maid, whose hands were stronger than mine, broke the cord, and my eyes immediately devoured the contents of the letter. Suddenly I let it drop from my hands, and my eyes filled with tears, so sad was the news it contained. In it my lord told me that the king had ordered him to command an escort which was to accompany a mission of the clergy to the court of the Holy Father at Rome; that his majesty had chosen him for the task, as he was, the king said, reputed one of the most pious knights at the court—an honour my dear husband, in his modesty, said he did not deserve, but which all who knew him said he justly merited.

So great was the sorrow this news gave my young heart—for then I was little more than twenty years of age, being hardly eighteen when I married—that I could not finish reading the letter for very tears, when my handmaiden, Bertha, told me there was more in it than I had seen; so I tried to read the remainder, but I cried so fast I could not. I would have asked Bertha to read it, as I had no secrets from her; but the poor girl was unlearned and could not, so I was obliged to dry my tears and control my feelings till I should finish it. Before I came to the end, I found my dear lord had requested me in it to take with me a sufficient escort and join him in London.

As soon as I had understood my lord's wish, I gave immediate orders for my departure; but they told me it was getting late in the day, and it would not be possible to have all in readiness before the morrow; but I was resolved, and made them, in spite of their unwillingness, obey me. Thinking it would please my lord, I also ordered the priest of our chapel to accompany me; but he made so many excuses about the unsafe state of the roads, that they were infested by disbanded soldiers from the wars, who were worse than even robbers, and that we should not arrive at Basingstoke before midnight. I was so ashamed of his cowardice, when my lord's wife required him to accompany her, that I was fain to leave him in disgust; but Bertha, who had no dread of him, but great love for me, said it was a grievous shame to find a priest so cowardly, and that he was unworthy of the confidence my lord reposed in him. This so shamed the man that he forthwith saddled his mule, and was ready for departure as soon as any of the others.

We started about three in the afternoon. As it was in the month of July, the days were long, and we had made good progress on our road before it was dark, yet, nevertheless, with all our speed we did not reach Basingstoke till one hour after midnight. It appeared strange to all the others that I, unaccustomed to bear fatigue, and having travelled but little, should have been less tired than any of my people, and still more strange that I, naturally timid, had shewn no signs of fear on the road, and yet there was, as I was then aware, although I would not own it, great danger from the wandering soldiers the priest had spoken of. I must also admit that, although he was much tired when we arrived at Basingstoke, possibly from his being a very infirm man, he shewed no symptoms of want of courage on the road.

The next day we started two hours before noon, and made so much haste that that night we slept at Kingston; and the next evening I had joined my dear lord, as he had directed me, at Crosby Palace.

When my lord saw me he lifted me from my palfry, and embraced me tenderly in the presence of all the knights who were standing around; yet I did not feel ashamed, he looked so noble and so manly. I felt it as an honour I was proud of, and I did not in any way blush at the gaze of those surrounding us. My lord then took me into a privy chamber, and told me to remain there while he went and asked permission of the king to accompany me to a house he had taken for me till he left England, which would not be before the end of August or middle of September, as the mission would not be ready before that time.

I cannot describe how happy I felt when I heard this. The idea of remaining with him so long was to me like a reprieve given to a man under sentence of death. It was like a year at any other time. As my lord passed under my window on his road to the king, I heard him tell our people not to take the horses away. In a short time my husband returned to me, and we left the chamber and descended into the courtyard, when he again placed me on my palfry, and, taking hold of the bridle, he led the horse himself, our people following us at a short distance.

My husband had taken a house for us near St Mary's Cross, outside Bishopgate. The house was small, indeed, when compared to our castle, but it was large enough for us, as our people, with the exception of the priest and Bertha and two other servants, were all lodged at a short distance from us. In this house we remained for five weeks, and I believe no part of my life—certainly my married life—was spent more happily than the quiet days we passed in that humble dwelling.

CHAPTER II.

BEFORE the time for my lord's departure arrived, the king gave a great feast to the courtiers, and I was invited to attend it. As my lord would in no way avoid an order of his liege sovereign, he requested me to obey the summons. I did so, not that I had any pleasure at the idea of being at the feast—for my heart was sad at my lord's approaching departure—nor altogether from the commands of his majesty, but simply that it was my duty, as a true and loving wife, to obey the wishes of my husband. Nor do I think my lord himself expected any pleasure at the feast, for his heart, like mine, was sad at the thought of our approaching separation.

The evening arrived, and I was presented for the first time both to the king and queen. They received me most graciously, and the king paid me many compliments on my beauty, which, in truth, were hardly due to me, but to Bertha, who had taken great pains with my dress, and made me very comely. But I could not tell the king so, and I said "his majesty was jesting with his poor servant;" but this he denied, and said that all he had told me was true. Although I felt honoured at all the compliments paid me before the courtiers, knights, and noble dames assembled round the throne, they gave me no delight; for I saw on the face of my dear husband that he was not pleased at the king's words; so I took an opportunity of mixing with the crowd as soon as I could do so without offence or rudeness to his majesty.

There was great feasting, dancing, and merriment that night, but I could not enjoy it. Many gay knights asked me to dance, but I had not the heart. My husband bade me have better spirits, and he brought to me as a partner in a dance a French nobleman, who was his friend and had lately arrived from Normandy. He was the Baron de Crevecour, Vidame of Beaujencey. He was a handsome, fine-looking man, of very noble appearance, and very richly dressed; but still I would not dance. My lord begged that I would, for he said if I did not, the Vidame would go back to Normandy with but a poor opinion of our English ladies, and that I did my countrywomen injustice. Still I had not spirit, and I begged the Vidame he would hold me excused, that it was not from rudeness on my part, but that I was in bad disposition for dancing.

The Vidame, with much courtesy, said he was sorry for my indisposition, and hoped another time he might be more fortunate. Several others asked me to dance, but I would not, and I was most thankful when my lord told me that the king and queen had retired, and that we could go home.

My lord spake but little on the road to our house. For this I was thankful, as without reason a certain sorrowful feeling oppressed me which I could not account for, and I felt that if he spoke kindly to me I should foolishly cry. When we had entered our sleeping chamber, he said to me—

"Sweet one, you did wrong not to dance with the Vidame. He will think it churlish of you, and speak of you when he goes back to Normandy as one not accustomed to courtly society."

I answered him—"My dear lord, it grieves me that I did not, but I had all the night so sorrowful a heart that I had no courage to dance."

"What ailed you, sweet one?" he said.

"I cannot tell," I answered, "but all the time a weight oppressed my spirits as if some terrible misfortune hung over us we could not avert. I think I am not well, for I had no cause whatever for the feeling."

"You think, love," he said, "too much of our separation. It will, be assured, last only a few months, and then I shall return to you. Come, come, do not cry, my sweet one; do not cry."

But I could not help it. He clasped me in his arms, and though I felt happy in his embrace, yet I still cried as I leant my head upon his breast. He placed his hand upon my head, and gently moved it from him so that he could see my face. I tried to conceal my feelings, and when I looked at him I smiled, but the tears ran down my face the while, and I behaved so foolishly, laughing and crying, that I wonder my dear lord had not been angry with me. Before undressing for bed I knelt before the image of the Virgin in our room, and prayed that she would take us in her holy keeping, and guard, especially, my dear husband from harm; likewise that she would keep him from anger at my silly behaviour, and give me more control over my feelings. But, alas! that night she did not grant me my last prayer; and in the end my husband chided me roundly and deservedly for my absurd, unreasoning behaviour.

The next day the fit had passed over, and my dear lord, who could not bear anger against me, loved me as dearly as ever. We walked happily and lovingly together in the fields around us, nor did we think of returning till we had arrived nearly at Bow. We were out many hours, yet so pleasingly did the time pass, that I felt, although unaccustomed to exercise of the kind, neither hunger nor fatigue, and could have walked still farther with equal pleasure, but my dear lord said that the autumn evening was too cold for me, and that we had better go home. We supped quietly together that night, and I could not help comparing the tranquil happiness we then enjoyed to the splendid sorrow of the court feast.

The term for my lord's departure rapidly approached, and my sorrow increased as the day drew near. He wished me to return home before he left England; but I pleaded so warmly that I might be allowed not only to remain with him, but to accompany him on his journey as far as Dover, that at last he granted my request. It was not without some difficulty, however, that I obtained it, for he feared greatly the dangers that I might experience in returning home alone; but I not only shewed him that Bertha would be with me, as well as the four stout men-at-arms who were to have formed my escort from London to the Castle, but also the priest who had accompanied me, who, now that his objection to travel was over, shewed me great attention. Moreover, his personal selfishness apart, he was a learned, pious man, and one on whom my dear lord could not only count for godly and good counsel for me, but great shrewdness and knowledge of the world as well.

At last all things were in readiness for his departure. The heavy baggage had been sent on some days before on mules and pack horses, so that the cavalcade could travel more at its ease. We left Crosby Palace, where we had assembled early in the morning of a fine autumn day. The party consisted of two bishops on mules, and their chaplains and servants and several sumpter horses and mules, so that we made a great show; my husband and the ten men-at-arms that were to form the escort of the mission, myself and Bertha, our chaplain, and the four men-at-arms who were to guard me home. The king graciously presented himself to the cavalcade before it left the palace gates, and wished us God speed and good success. He also saw me and asked me if I was to accompany my lord, as, if so, he should be sorry, as I was an ornament to the court. I was glad my dear lord did not hear the king's remark, as it might have displeased him, and it would have pained me greatly had anything occurred which would have caused him anger and be on the eve of leaving me. I told the king that I was only to accompany my lord as far as Dover, and that then I should return to the castle. He inquired if I should pass through London? I informed him that was my lord's order, but that I should remain only two or three days—the time, in fact, sufficient to collect our servants and chattels, and that I should remain at the castle till my lord's return. "Not so, pretty mistress," he said, "I shall lie in wait for you, and detain you for the service of our queen." When he had said this, one of the bishops addressed him, and I was well pleased that I could leave him without offence and mingle with the rest. I was sadly in doubt whether I should tell my lord these remarks of the king's, and I reflected on it for some time; but at last I bethought me that it might be, and most certainly was, only a joke on the part of the king, and that probably if I told it to my husband as having been said in earnest, it might cause him pain or displeasure. So I determined on not mentioning it to my lord, a folly I have often bitterly repented since.

At last the cavalcade started, and a brilliant sight we made in the morning's sun as we passed down Gracechurch Street. As we crossed the bridge, the dwellers in the houses on each side rushed to their doors, and asked for the blessings of the bishops as we passed, which were immediately and most willingly given. When we had arrived in Southwark, the Lord Bishop of Winchester with great goodness left his palace to meet us. When we saw him the cavalcade halted, and he conversed for some short time with the bishops in the mission, and then giving them, and afterwards the whole cavalcade, his benediction, he passed on.

We rested that night at Rochester, where we were received into the castle and hospitably treated by the governor, that is to say, the bishops and their chaplains, my lord, myself, and Bertha, but the rest were lodged close by in the town. We had had, however, little enjoyment of our evening meal, being much fatigued by our journey, although the weather had been fine. The next morning the bishop called upon us just before we started, and invited us to rest the day with him; but the envoys told him they could not, as they were that evening to meet some other of the clergy and a secretary who were to join the mission at Canterbury, where we were to rest that evening. To this the bishop replied that he had that morning received notice that the clergy we spoke of, with the secretary, had left Canterbury for Dover yesterday, where they would await us even if it should be a week before we overtook them, so there was now no impediment against our remaining at Rochester for the day.

After the mission had duly considered his hospitable offer, they decided that as all things were ready for the journey they had better go on; so thanking the Bishop of Rochester for his proffered hospitality, they left him and continued on their way.

That evening we slept in Canterbury. The next morning the mission determined that, although the others had gone on to Dover, they would remain the two days proposed in Canterbury, not only that they had some affairs to transact with the brethren of the Augustine monastery, but also that the next day being Sunday and the feast day of the Blessed Saint Michael the Archangel, they determined on hearing high mass before encountering the perils of their journey both by sea and land. This determination gave great joy to my dear lord, for, as I have before said, he was very pious and took great delight in all the high ceremonies of the Church; and, I believe, had it not been for his great wish to be present and witness some of the grand functions of our Holy Mother Church at Rome, as well as to receive the Benediction of his Holiness, not even the king's command, unless most authoritatively expressed, would have induced him to leave me.

In the morning of Saturday we occupied ourselves in visiting the town and its holy places, and in the afternoon we attended in the chapel of the Blessed St Thomas the Martyr in the cathedral, to hear a mass which had been desired by my noble lord for the welfare of his soul and his safe return, and also that we might meet again in good health and happiness. He also ordained that two masses for the same end should be said on my return, at which I was to be present, for all of which he made a liberal offering, to the great content of the priest and the benefit of his own soul.

The next day being a feast-day and Sunday, we attended high mass. Never had I seen the august mysteries of our holy Church conducted with so much splendour—truly, I thought, what God is equal to our God, or what religion so beautiful as our own? My dear husband during the whole time knelt by my side, and many times did I look at him and thank God who had given me so noble and beauteous a man for a husband. We afterwards attended vespers together, and in the evening we went early to bed.

The next morning was to be our last before his departure. We had received notice that the tide would serve in the afternoon, and that we must without fail be in Dover four hours before sunset. We started off early, and proceeded leisurely along. Our pace this day was slow and lingering. No one in the cavalcade seemed happy, why I know not. Perhaps my own sad thoughts made me think that all looked sad likewise. But slow as was the pace of the cavalcade, my lord's and mine were slower, and by degrees we dropped considerably behind the others—even Bertha was far in advance of us. I wanted him to speak, yet he said nothing, nor had I the heart to talk myself. Onward we continued our slow pace, mile after mile, but not a word was uttered by either, yet both understood each other, for we both knew it was the love that we bore each other that occupied our thoughts the while we were silent. We continued thus till Dover Castle was in sight, when my dear husband seemed to wake to the realities of the world, and with a deep sigh, which seemed to come from the bottom of his heart, he told me to give my palfrey the spur, and we overtook the others before they had arrived at the port.

When we were by the sea-shore we found those whom we expected to meet in Canterbury had already embarked on board the ship, which was a short distance from the land, as well as the luggage we had sent on a few days previous. The embarkation of our party then took place in the boats, and all were put on board without accident, my dear husband standing by me the while, giving his orders and seeing that all was done with proper despatch and regularity. When it came to his turn to enter the boat, he first clasped me in his arms and imprinted one long kiss of love on my lips; he then stepped into the boat and seated himself in the stern. As the rowers began to ply their oars, he turned round and cast on me a look so full of sadness and love that it thrilled to my very heart. Never have I forgotten that look, and for weeks after his departure it was perpetually recurring to my memory. He did not alter his position till the boat had reached the ship, nor did I move from the spot he had left me on till the ship had sailed and was fading on the sight. Then, weeping and broken-hearted, the priest and a man-at-arms of my party conducted me to the castle, where the governor, aware of my arrival, had made preparations for my reception, and that of Bertha and the priest, for the night.

The next morning I found myself very sad and lonely. The weather had changed, and I could hear the wind howling round my casement, and the sea roaring in the distance. I began trembling for my dear lord, thinking that he might not yet be arrived in Calais, and that he might be in peril of shipwreck; whereupon I went on my knees and offered up a prayer to the Virgin to hold him in her holy keeping and protect him in all danger. I then felt calmer, and I commenced dressing myself for my journey, Bertha assisting me.

While we were thus occupied I heard two voices talking under my casement. One was the voice of my priest, the other I had heard before, but I could not remember when or in what place. I did not hear all they were talking about, but the latter voice, in part of the conversation, feelingly said—" How sad that one so good, so young, so lovely, should be left without protection!"

" In truth it is," said the priest; "but I trust that God and the blessed Virgin will take her in their holy keeping."

To which the other devoutly said—" Amen."

I asked Bertha whose the other voice might be, but she said she did not know, nor had she seen any one likely to have made the remark. I was on the point of telling the girl to go and see, but then I remembered that such an act would be unseemly on my part, and that, now my dear lord had left me, it behoved me that in all things, however small, my behaviour should be regulated with all severity and strictness, even in appearance; so I said nothing. Shortly afterwards the priest informed me that all was ready for my journey; so, thanking the governor of the castle for the hospitality he had given me, I bade him good-day, and we started on our homeward journey.

We arrived that evening in Canterbury. During the day the weather had been stormy, and my fears at first were aroused that my dear husband might be in danger; but the

A Legend of Wilton Abbey. 19

leader of the men-at-arms, who had himself formerly been a seaman, told me that the wind, although strong, was quite favourable, and that my dear lord had arrived in Calais but a few hours after he had left Dover. As the man seemed to speak with experience and truth, his words gave me great comfort, and I went on my way less sadly than before.

My sleep that night was something more peaceable than the night before; still I woke often, and wished that the day would come, for I hoped to receive great consolation from attending the masses that my husband had requested should be said.

The next day I attended at the appointed time in the chapel of the holy Saint Thomas to hear the mass. During the celebration I prayed fervently that both our lives might be in his holy guidance and protection, and that we might have a happy and early meeting.

During the service once, on rising from my knees, my eyes rested on a worshipper who prayed in the same chapel. He was at some distance from me, and it seemed as if his figure was not unknown to me; but his face I did not see, as his head was bent forwards as if in deep prayer. I thought no more of it, my mind being immediately afterwards absorbed in my devotions. When the service was over I remained some time longer in the chapel on my knees; but the priest who had accompanied me, as well as Bertha, had left it. When I rose I found them standing near the grand entrance-door, and the priest was in conversation with the stranger whom I had seen in the chapel. When I joined them, to my great surprise I found the stranger was the Baron de Crevecour, Vidame of Beaujencey. He made me a low obeisance when he saw me, and, with sorrow on his countenance, he offered me the asperges brush that I might touch the holy water on it as I left the church. I thought as I crossed myself that it was a pleasing sight to see so noble a gentleman so attentive to the ordinances and ceremonies of religion, the more so as I knew that many of the courtiers were profligate and profane men.

In the evening I asked our chaplain if he knew the Vidame. He told me he had seen him once or twice in London, and he had that morning met him in the castle. The Vidame, he said, had been to Dover with those of the mission who were to have joined us at Canterbury; that he was near me when my lord embarked, but that, marking my great sorrow, he had thought it would be an indiscretion on his part to attempt to console me, although, from my grief, he was much tempted.

He further told me the Vidame would proceed toward London the next day with two aged ecclesiastics, his relatives, and that he intended presenting himself to me that evening, if I would allow him, to ask permission to profit by my escort, as his two relatives were infirm, and very timorous as well, and they were afraid of meeting bad characters on the road.

The Vidame called on me, as the priest had foretold, with one of his relatives, an aged and infirm man, and asked the protection of my escort. This I readily promised, as in the company of two such holy men as the priests there could be no suspicion of scandal with respect to the Vidame; but even then I would not have accorded it had it not been true that the road was most dangerous from the robbers that infested it, and who had but little regard for our Holy Church or its servants.

Our journey from Canterbury to Rochester the next day would have been a happy one, could my dear lord have been with me. We discoursed, the Vidame and myself, with the priests, not only upon holy things, but upon the beauty of nature and many other subjects, which lightened our fatigue, and made the road seem shorter. When we arrived in

Rochester the governor again hospitably received me. The Vidame and his relatives rested at the bishop's palace.

The next day we proceeded on to London. The journey would have passed as smoothly as the day before, had it not been that the distance was so much longer, and, in consequence, the fatigue greater. When, towards the evening, the Vidame noticed that I was much tired, he attempted to beguile the way by telling me of different countries he had visited, and what manner of people inhabited them. I found also, to my great satisfaction, that he had remained some months in Rome, and knew many people there. I asked him many questions, all of which he readily answered; and more than that, he spoke of the beauty of the Roman ladies, but that they were little to be respected, being in every one's opinion very light of character.

Seeing I had no pleasure in such conversation, he changed she subject, and told me about his barony in Normandy, and the rich abbey near it of Beaujencey. I also found the father abbot held him in great favour; and having noticed his respect for holy things and all ministries of the Church, he had appointed him Vidame (which with us would signify captain) of the troops the abbey was obliged to furnish to the king for the estates it held, and of which no ecclesiastic could, with proper respect for religion, take the direct command. All this raised the Vidame in my opinion; in truth I had not ever met with so gallant a gentleman who was so piously inclined.

The Vidame and his relatives left me soon after we had entered Southwark, as they were to be lodged in the palace or the Bishop of Winchester, but we continued our way over the bridge. Before our companions left us the two priests thanked me greatly for the protection my escort had afforded them, and the Vidame thanked me also for allowing him to ride in my society. I much feared he would have proposed to call on me, and I should not have known what answer to return him, for I would not allow him or any other gallant cavalier willingly to enter my house while my lord was away; but he had behaved to me with so much courtesy that it would have pained me to refuse him. Fortunately he said nothing, and I respected him the more for his silence.

CHAPTER III.

THE next morning, when I was busy giving orders to my servants touching the manner of my departure from London, and in what way every thing should be arranged, I heard a noise of many men and horses approaching the house. Presently I heard a great sound of trumpets, and then suddenly all was silent, and the cavalcade halted in front of our house. One of my men-at-arms, to gratify his curiosity, went to open the gate, but fortunately before doing so he looked through the little wicket and saw many gay knights, together with the king at their head, waiting without. The man was startled at so much splendour, and ran back to the house saying what he had seen. Although I was very much frightened at this visit from the king, I was in one way glad that my man-at-arms had given me notice, for my dress was such as I would not willingly receive any one in, still less the king. I ran to my chamber, and, calling Bertha, I quickly changed my dress, so quickly indeed that I wondered afterwards at the haste I had made.

In the meantime the grooms had knocked several times at the outer gate, and now, being ready, I ordered a man-at-arms to open it. The king and one or two knights rode in, and the others remained outside. I went, as in duty bound, to the front door to receive the king, and thank him for doing my humble dwelling so much honour, though at the time in my heart I wished him far away.

He dismounted from his horse and entered the hall, and

there he graciously requested me to take a seat; and he also seated himself on a stool at the same time—the two knights with him remained the while standing.

"So, pretty mistress," said the king to me, "you are come back to us again. By my faith I am glad of it. We shall now add another beauty to the ladies of our queen, and one that will go far to outshine them all."

I told the king that my husband had desired me to leave London for the castle as soon as might be after his departure, and that I hoped his majesty would excuse me.

"That indeed I will not," he said; "why, what a traitor is your lord when he knew his king's pleasure on the subject!" (This he said laughing, well knowing how readily my lord obeyed him in all things.) "But I love him after all, and would guard from all harm his pretty wife. Where could he find her more securely placed than with the ladies of the queen?"

I was so much embarrassed I knew not what to answer. I wished to obey my husband, and yet (so much did he honour the king, and such respect did he pay to his wishes,) I doubted whether I ought to refuse. After reflecting a moment, I said that I still hoped his majesty would hold me excused; but that if he would not, I could not, from the respect it was my duty to bear him, do other than accept the honour he offered me.

"That was spoken," said the king, "like a wise lady, and the wife of a loyal nobleman. Why, how could he be so selfish as to wish his pretty wife to remain shut up in his castle while he amuses himself in Italy? And let me tell you that you are a lady of great courage to allow your husband to remain so long in Rome. You do not know those Roman dames. The handsome Englishman, your husband, will not want admirers among them, or they differ from their reputation."

Here the king laughed heartily at his own wit, and his two knights still more heartily than he. I was so annoyed at the way the king spoke of my dear husband that, had it not been for the respect it was my duty to shew him, I should have told him to leave the house. I dared not display any anger to the king, but I rewarded the two knights with such a look of displeasure for their impertinence that it did not escape them. The king also noticed my look, and rebuked the knights for their behaviour, for though he would behave rudely himself he would not allow it in others.

When he had done speaking to the knights, he said to me, "To-morrow, pretty mistress, the queen will expect you. Do not disappoint her."

Then he and his knights, to my great contentment, left the house.

When I began to think over the king's visit, I became thoroughly uneasy and miserable. In the first place, I did not know whether I had done rightly to accept the king's offer. Oh! how I regretted that I had not told my dear lord the words of the king the morning of the departure of the mission. I thought his majesty had been in jest, or I should have told him all. Again, I felt angry at the remarks the king had made about the Roman ladies. Why should he tell me that? What cared I whether the Roman ladies were beautiful or ugly, virtuous or frail? Did he think that I feared for my noble lord? Did he think he could shake my faith in him? No, he was as honest in his love as the day, and never for a moment would I doubt him; yet still— yet still—I felt uneasy, and I sat myself on a stool and wept bitterly without knowing why.

The next day I made Bertha dress me very carefully, and before noon I presented myself at the palace, and was shortly afterwards ushered into the presence of the queen. Her majesty received me very kindly, and talked with me a long time, sometimes about my dear husband and sometimes about myself. She said my dear lord was a good man, and that I was fortunate in having such a husband, and she was sure he had also a good wife. Her voice was so gentle and her manner so kind that tears almost came into my eyes with the pleasure that she gave me, and I thought how different were my feelings that day to what they were the day before when the king spoke so slightingly about my husband and the Roman ladies. Before my interview with the queen had ended the king came into the chamber, and seemed much pleased to see me, and behaved kindly to me, without that rude joking he had used the day before, and I fully forgave him the pain he had given me.

Before I left the palace the queen told me she wished me to act as one of her ladies. I was thinking what answer to make her when the king, noticing my embarrassment, said—

"She is afraid her husband will not like her remaining at the Court. But I will arrange all. She shall stay with us till she hears from him on the subject, which will not take a long time, as a messenger will leave to-morrow to overtake, if possible, the mission before it arrives in Rome, and she can send a letter by him to ask his permission. And the queen," he said, "will also send a letter asking his permission, so we need not fear the answer."

The possibility of sending a letter to my dear lord, and so soon having his reply, decided me on obeying her majesty, at which she expressed herself much pleased, and told me to take my place with the other ladies of honour as soon as I conveniently could. I then left the palace and returned home, not discontented with the turn the affair had taken.

I wrote my letter to my dear lord, concealing nothing, and asking him to give me his explicit orders how I should conduct myself, and I would faithfully obey his wishes like a good, loving, and dutiful wife. I then gave it to the messenger, and that he might not fail to deliver it I rewarded him liberally.

In a few days afterwards I joined the queen's ladies of honour. As we waited on her person on all state occasions, I saw a great many people, and among them some of the first lords of the land. I also saw with pleasure the Vidame at the court. I say with pleasure, for he behaved with so much modesty and reserve, and in the frequent interviews with him which chance threw in my way, never on any occasion did he presume on his opportunity, so that I had no fear in addressing him whenever I met him. His behaviour was the more remarkable, as the king and his courtiers in general placed little restraint upon themselves, but sometimes talked so openly that it pained me to hear them.

Although I saw the Vidame frequently, it was for some weeks always in the palace, but at last he attended at my house to bring me some news of my husband, (I had been confined to the house for some days from severe cold.) He asked me to pardon the liberty he had taken in calling on me without an invitation, but, knowing the anxiety I was in about the safe arrival of my husband, he thought the news he had received would be acceptable to me. It was, that my husband and the whole of the mission had arrived safely at Viterbo. He expected to hear more in a few days, and, if I wished it, he would call on me with whatever news he might have. As my cold did not improve very rapidly, I accepted his offer with thanks, and after he had remained talking with me for more than half an hour, he left my house.

The more I saw of the Vidame the more amiable he appeared, and I began to entertain a sincere friendship for him. I was not altogether sorry he had called on me, although it was against the rule I had established, that no gentleman should be allowed to visit at the house during my lord's absence. Our chaplain, to whom I generally looked for advice and good counsel, had lately become so irritable from his severe asthma, that I did not like asking him any questions, and I could now, if need be, apply to the Vidame. I could do so the more readily as he was not forward, free, or unmannerly in his way of addressing me, but modest and reserved. At the same time I perceived he took great interest in all that concerned me, without priding himself on any little service he rendered.

In a few days he called on me again, and this time he brought with him a letter from my lord, which had arrived by the same messenger who had been charged with my letter. I opened my lord's letter in the presence of the Vidame, to whom I excused myself, as being anxious to see that my lord was well; but he said he could inform me of the fact, for the messenger had told him he had seen my lord more than once, and that he was in perfect health, and appeared very happy. I do not know why I should have felt vexed that my husband was very happy, but certainly I little liked the news, but I did not let my annoyance appear to the Vidame.

Hearing my lord was in good health, I put the letter aside to read it when I should be alone, and I remained talking with the Vidame, who this time remained longer than before. When he had gone I read my lord's letter, in which he gave me an account of his travels and adventures, and also sent me many sweet remembrances and kind loves, which did not please me so much as they might have done, as I remembered how happy he was, as the Vidame had told me. One thing, however, in his letter pleased me and gave me great satisfaction. He told me I had done right in obeying the order of the queen to be one of her ladies of honour. He also advised me to keep in the small house I was living in, and only to be at the palace when my duty required it. All this pleased me exceedingly, and before I laid my head on my pillow that night, not only was the fact of my husband being so happy forgiven, but it seemed almost forgotten by me as well.

The Vidame now came frequently to visit me, and I felt pleasure in seeing him. His behaviour still continued most respectful in every way, and my confidence in him increased. True, his conversation did not so often turn on godly subjects as it was wont when first I knew him, and he was more witty and gay, but still not a word did he utter that I even could have objected to. I was also happier myself, for my anxiety about my dear lord had passed; as I more than once heard, indirectly, through the Vidame, that my lord was well and very happy, which last now did not vex me so much as it had done at first.

About this time a circumstance occurred which gave me great annoyance. Bertha, one day, was so impertinent to me, that I resolved to send her into the country. I was naturally very fond of the girl—she was my foster sister— and I allowed her to be more free with me in conversation than ladies ordinarily allow their servants. But the girl encroached upon my condescension, and frequently interfered in things which did not concern her and which were above her. She had been sullen and froward for some time past, and on more than one occasion very uncivil to the Vidame, whom she pretended greatly to dislike. I well understood the reason of her behaviour. When our chaplain became too infirm to counsel me, she hoped I should be guided by her, but it was not likely I should take advice from a menial, and one not older than myself. She therefore got jealous of my requesting on more than one occasion the opinion of the Vidame. She first commenced her impertinence by tossing up her head when he came into the room; when he spoke to her she pretended not to hear him, and when she had to fetch anything for him, (for she generally stopped in the chamber with us,) she would do it with a flounce as if it were against her wish.

I did not like to speak to her about it, as I feared I might receive some impertinent reply; but one day when she had been particularly uncivil to the Vidame, I took occasion, after his departure, to lecture her on her behaviour. She took my remarks in high dudgeon, and rudely said, she thought the Vidame came far oftener than there was any occasion for.

I was naturally most indignant at the insult contained in this most impertinent answer. Never was one more unjust. No human being could have been more respectful in his behaviour than the Vidame had been to me. A brother could not have been purer in his attention than that worthy nobleman.

"How dare you," I said, "you base girl, speak thus of so honourable a gentleman. If you ever repeat such a remark, that moment I will send you back in disgrace to your mother."

The bold thing, instead of being frightened at my remark, stood undaunted before me.

"I will say it again," she said; "he comes here too often, and he is not an honourable gentleman."

I was thunderstruck at her audacity. I told her that it was infamous in a menial to speak so of a gentleman of high degree, and if she were not silent I would send her home.

"I will not be silent," she said; "he is not an honourable gentleman, and I know it."

"What do you know of him?" I inquired.

"That everybody says he is a base, profligate man, and a great hypocrite."

"Were he not a good and pious man," I condescendingly argued, "he would not have been chosen to command the soldiers of the abbey."

"He was chosen, it is true, because from his hypocrisy they believed him to be worthy; but he was soon found out and dismissed, and he does not now command them."

"For what was he dismissed?" I inquired, as if to mistrust her statement.

"For his profligate behaviour, not only with a married lady, but with a nun as well."

I was astounded at the girl's statement, and was silent for some time. I was so enraged at her that I felt my eyes glared at her, and I could not speak. At last I was no longer mistress of myself, and I raised my hand and struck her.

She then burst into tears, and her passion got the better of her,—"It is true as heaven," said she, "and I heard from those who would not deceive me; and this I will say, that he comes here more often than my honoured master would like if he knew it."

This remark of the thoughtless, passionate girl terminated all between us. It was unpardonable. No woman could hold her husband more scrupulously in respect than I did my dear lord. Not one thought to his dishonour had ever crossed my mind, nor had one word, even in allusion, ever passed the lips of the Vidame in my presence that an honest wife might not have heard, or the most jealous husband known without thought of suspicion arising from it. The insult had deeply stung me, and I ordered Bertha immediately to prepare herself for her journey homewards, and as soon as she was ready to leave my house and reside with the wife of my lord's headman, who lived close by us, till I had an opportunity to send her under proper escort home. She made no reply, but without hesitation obeyed me, and in less than half an hour had left the house.

After she had gone I began tranquilly to think over what had passed between us. I felt, I am sorry to say, less annoyed at the slight she insinuated I had offered to my lord, in allowing the Vidame to visit me, than at what she had told me she had heard of his profligate life, and the statements she had made respecting the cause of his being dismissed from the command of the abbot's men-at-arms. I could not for a moment believe it to be otherwise than a gross slander on that noble gentleman's character by some one jealous of his good qualities. Still, her words annoyed me more than with justice they ought to have done, without my being able to satisfy myself with a reason for the feeling. I determined at last that, when the Vidame arrived, I would question him on the subject, and if he did not clear it up in a satisfactory manner, it would only be a proper mark of respect to my husband, on my part, to dismiss him the house and refuse to admit him again. My resolution once taken, I calmly awaited the hour of his visit.

When the Vidame arrived, he was ushered into the room in which I was seated. We were then alone, as I had no woman servant in the house that I could raise to the position Bertha had occupied. The Vidame perceived from my countenance that something had angered me, but he was too discreet to inquire the cause. I was somewhat puzzled how to commence the conversation. I wished to express myself calmly, and begin by telling him that I had been obliged to dismiss Bertha, and then by degrees arrive at the cause of his dismissal from the post of captain of the abbot's men-at-arms, and afterwards inquire into the truth of her statement; but I had no sooner commenced than an uncontrollable power seemed to seize me, and I abruptly and angrily demanded if Bertha's statement of his profligacy were true?

The Vidame listened to me at first with great astonishment, then with profound sorrow. It was some moments after I had finished before he could find words to reply. When he spoke, intense grief seemed almost to choke his utterance.

By degrees he recovered himself, and then with dignity and emotion repudiated the base slander. His character, he said, was unsullied by any of the gross imputations I had heard. He had not been dismissed from the command of the abbot's men-at-arms; he had resigned the appointment from his own good will. If I doubted his statement, it could be confirmed by my writing to his two aged relatives whom I had seen on the journey from Dover, but who had now returned to Normandy. He would, he continued, disguise nothing from me, but give me candidly his reason for leaving France. He did not claim for himself any exemption from human frailty; he confessed few men could love more ardently than he. He loved but seldom, but then warmly and faithfully.

A lady, he said, the wife of a baron residing near the abbey, had fallen in love with him; but he bore her no affection, and as he had no taste for frivolous dalliance where the heart had no part, he thought it better to leave Normandy for a season and let her unhappy passion die away. This, he supposed, was the original of the report Bertha had heard, and which she had greatly exaggerated. The story about the nun he repudiated with indignation. He had too much respect for the sanctity of the cloister, and things holy in general, to be capable of so infamous an action.

I was fully satisfied with his explanation. He had given it in that frank, courtly, and noble manner which carried conviction with it. I told him candidly his statement gave me pleasure and satisfaction. I also mentioned, that as I had sent Bertha away, and that none other of my women was fit to fill her place, his remaining longer might appear unfavourably to others, and I trusted he would excuse my requesting him to leave.

He readily acquiesced. When he rose, he hoped, he said, that when he came next time I should have found another maiden to my taste. I told him I feared I should not, as I was somewhat difficult to please, and to find one easily who knew her duty was a hard matter.

As he was leaving he turned to me and said that a French noble lady of his acquaintance had a maiden who wished to leave her. He feared the lady was to blame, who was most irritable in her temper, but an honourable lady all the same. He said he would inquire of her, if I pleased, whether the maiden was still in England; and if so, he would send her to me, and I could judge if she would suit me. He did not know the girl himself—he doubted if he had ever seen her.

I willingly accepted his offer. I had long wished to have by me a French maiden, as they were more expert in dressing their mistresses than our clumsier English girls. I requested the Vidame to send her to me the next morning, and he promised he would do so if he could find her. He then took his leave, and I was well contented with the explanation he had given me.

The next morning the French serving-girl called on me, and pleased me much. She told me the countess she served at present was naturally a good lady, but so passionate that she would strike a servant that had displeased her; and as she herself had been threatened more than once, she would not remain. She hoped I would take her into my service, as she was sure I was an amiable lady, who would treat no servant so unkindly. This made me think of Bertha, and I blushed; but the French girl did not notice it.

I told her I would call that afternoon on the countess, and if I found she had told me the truth I would certainly engage her. She thanked me very gracefully for my kindness and left me. I called on the French countess, whose appearance I did not like. She spoke very well of the girl, and I determined to take her, and told her so when I left the house; and she promised to come to me the next morning, at which I was very glad, as I missed Bertha exceedingly.

CHAPTER IV.

WAS soon reconciled for the loss of Bertha, whom I had sent into the country. The French maiden pleased me greatly. She was quick, good-humoured, ready-witted, and skilful in dressing me. She also liked the Vidame, whom she only knew by sight, she said, but she knew all his relatives in Normandy personally, and the Vidame by reputation. She was always fond of talking of things which had taken place in France, and in which the Vidame had part. She spoke also of his great courage and generous disposition, but that it was a great pity he was not rich. I questioned her about the stories Bertha had told me, and she said they were false as far as regarded the nun. The story, as told by the Vidame, about the wife of the baron was true—that she had fallen in love with the Vidame, but he would not love her in return. As the baron was his friend, he thought it would be more honourable for him to leave Normandy, so he gave up his appointment as captain of the abbot's men-at-arms.

I was much pleased at all this, as I could now have the Vidame's society without scandal. He came in the afternoon very often, but I always kept my French servant in the room with us as far as I could without giving umbrage. When first the girl came she was wont to leave the room, but I chided her for it; and she now remained with us, occasionally leaving us on business of her own.

As this is my confession, I will do it with an honest heart, painful as it is to me. I am now entering on my tale of sin and sorrow. My iniquity dated from my quarrel with Bertha. When she had left me I grew careless, knowing no one overlooked me, our poor old priest being laid on a bed of sickness through asthma. My French maid always agreed with me, and was ever in advance in her praises of the Vidame. The thoughts of my dear lord were far less frequently in my mind than they used to be, while those of the Vidame became more frequent, and I had greater pleasure in his society. Let me not be misunderstood; not one thought directly derogatory to my dear lord had yet passed my brain, but still I can now trace I was already in the path of sin. The behaviour of the Vidame also was little to be blamed. True, he was far more gay than formerly, and was sometimes very merry and joyous, but at others he appeared very sad.

All things went on quietly till the king ordered a great feast to be given on Christmas Eve, and I and the Vidame were among the guests invited. It was to be very gay, and there was to be much dancing and merriment. I confess the news gave me great joy, and I promised myself much mirth and pleasure, especially as my friend the Vidame was to be there also.

Therès, my servant, made me that evening look very handsome, and I was well content with the figure I made. I arrived at the palace at an early hour, but still the Vidame was before me. He seemed delighted with my appearance, and his praise made me more content with myself than ever. We discoursed very pleasantly together till other guests arrived, and when the king and queen made their appearance dancing began. I danced with the Vidame, who danced beautifully; and all complimented us on our performance. I afterwards danced with an English knight, whereat the Vidame looked most sorrowful all the time, and I was sore vexed with myself for having offended him. The next dance I danced with him, and he seemed happy again, and told me he was grateful to me for my kindness. I danced also several other times with him before supper.

It was midnight before the supper was ready. The Vidame seated himself beside me; and all was mirth and gaiety, and the time passed most merrily along. I was thoroughly happy. The Vidame talked only with me, and I saw jealousy in the faces of the other ladies to think that so handsome and gallant a cavalier should hold no converse with them; but I liked him the better for it.

When the supper was over, although we were far advanced in the morn of the Holy Nativity, we again went into the dancing-room; but as many stood up to dance, the Vidame proposed that we should sit down, which we did on a seat apart from the rest. While talking thus, he for the first time forgot the respect he owed me, and made love to me so warmly that, for a moment, I forgot my own and my lord's dignity, and listened to him; but the next I recovered myself and left the spot, shewing by my face that I was much offended. He followed me and sued for my pardon. He said he had been too bold, that his passion for me had made him forget himself, and that he had hitherto restrained his love. I would not hear him, but walked away indignantly.

Here let me pause to tell the sad truth. I was angry with him for the disrespect he shewed me, to think that I was a light of love; but I, as a woman, was flattered and pleased at the conquest I had made.

The Vidame followed me continually, imploring my forgiveness, which I would not accord; and at last he seated himself, and I noticed the tears came into his eyes. My heart felt for him, but still I would not forgive him, but talked with others, and made belief I was happy, and would not notice him.

When the dancing was over, he again approached me, and begged I would hear one word from him. I listened. He said he had done wrongly, and he saw how great was his fault, and he had determined to absolve it.. He would that night destroy himself, for he could not live under my displeasure. He begged of me when he was no more at least then to pardon him, and with that knowledge he should die happy.

I was alarmed at his words, and told him the wickedness of his intention—for he was a bold man, and would certainly keep his promise. I believed he could not live under my displeasure, and I feared his blood would be on my head. Still I refused to forgive him, but more gently. I could not be really angry with him, he looked so noble in his sorrow. I thought it was wicked in me to have no mercy on him, and let him destroy himself. I glanced at his handsome countenance. I smiled kindly on him, and as I turned from him I offered him my hand in token of forgiveness.

I shrieked with terror! My hand had been gently pressed, but by no mortal fingers. The hand that had pressed mine was the cold, clammy, loathsome hand of a fast-mouldering corpse. Its cold poison numbed my arm, and in a moment pervaded my whole body with its nauseous power. I looked around me—no one was there who could have taken my hand, for at the moment we were by ourselves, and the Vidame, who had turned from me, had not noticed the pledge I had offered him.

The guests crowded round me, and plied me with questions, none of which I could answer; for the sickly sensation the horrid contact had caused me deprived me of the power of speech—still all looked at me with wonder. The Vidame approached me with alarm and surprise in his face. A knight advised that my litter should be sent for, and in a few moments it was ready. Fortunately neither the king nor the queen at the moment were in the hall, so they heard nothing.

The Vidame, assisted by one of the courtiers, conducted me to my litter. The Vidame asked me, with pity in his tone, if I felt better. I told him yes, but that my hand was still cold as ice. He held it for a moment in his, but it did not warm it; still the feeling relieved me, it was so different from the horrible sensation I had so lately felt. With some little difficulty I was helped into my litter, and the Vidame, walking by my side, accompanied me home.

The next day I kept my bed, for my soul was sick at the remembrance of the horrible feeling I had felt the night before. Towards evening it decreased, and before the morrow it had passed away, save when the memory of it returned strongly to me.

On the third day, when the Vidame's visit was announced, (my French maiden told me he had called each day twice, he was so anxious about me, but he had told her in no wise to let me know of it; but she could not, she said, keep a secret from me,) I allowed him to see me. When he came in he appeared so pale and so sorrowful for my illness, and the displeasure I had shewed him, that I forgave him fully in my heart for the affront he had offered me. He inquired what had ailed me at the feast, but I was so shocked at the horrible occurrence that I did not tell him, but found some excuse. I was also most thankful that I had kept it from all on the night it happened, and I now determined I would let no one know it.

The Vidame remained that day but a short time, as he feared, he said, to fatigue me. He spoke not of his presumptuous behaviour, nor did I. As I had forgiven him, I thought it would be ungenerous on my part to speak of it; and so I held my peace.

When I had fully recovered from the horrible shock I had received, I began to think calmly over in my mind what it might mean. At first I could come to no conclusion, but presently an idea presented itself to my mind, which I immediately drove away. Again and again it came, and so frequently, that at last, in spite of myself, I was obliged to consider it. It appeared to me a possible warning that my dear lord was dead. It did not have the effect on my mind that so terrible a misfortune would have been likely to occasion, for I could not realise a sorrow so great. Afterwards, when I looked at it more closely, I was astounded that it did not cause greater terror in my soul than it did; but I believed then, as I coolly and conscientiously now believe, with the full knowledge of my approaching end before me, that the uncertainty of my lord's death dimmed, to a considerable extent, the dreadful nature of such a disaster.

Days passed, and that misfortune which had only appeared possible now assumed so strong a probability that I began to anticipate the news almost as a certainty, when suddenly my conscience brought so clearly before me my infamous selfishness in not lamenting more the misfortune which had possibly befallen me, that I began to consider more attentively the state of my thoughts.

And when I did so, how shameful, how disgraceful was the result! Hardly a tear had I shed, not a prayer had I offered up to Heaven for the benefit of his soul if dead, or for his health, happiness, and safe guidance if alive. I admitted my infamy, I confessed my heartlessness, and prayed that I might be blessed with a proper state of mind; still my prayer was not answered. I felt terrified at the silence of Heaven to my prayer, but I saw on further investigation that my supplication to Heaven had not been made with that earnestness of heart which alone can deserve acceptation. I determined that I would diligently investigate the state of my conscience, and then make a further appeal. I first brought vividly to my mind all the noble qualities of my husband, and I proved to myself how grateful I ought to have been to

Heaven for making me the wife of such a worthy gentleman, and how greatly I ought to sorrow for his loss. I then appealed to Heaven for the love I ought to shew his memory, for I innately felt the certainty of his death;—still no answer to my prayer. I then proposed to myself to confess, and follow strictly the advice of the priest; but singular to say that I, who hitherto had found such comfort at the confessional, now could not bring my resolution to appeal to it.

At last I was obliged to admit the truth that I had hitherto attempted with all my ingenuity to conceal from myself. It was not alone the doubt of his death which caused this apathy —for I felt he was in heaven—but the certainty that I, sinner that I was, loved another.

I shut myself from the world. I saw no one but the man I ought not to have seen, and him but seldom. I reflected on the miracle which had occurred to me at the king's feast, and tried to persuade myself it was a message from my husband that he was no more, so that my sin in feeling affection for the Vidame might be lessened; but I still avoided seeking the aid of the confessional to direct me in my dilemma.

A messenger arrived from Rome, but brought no letter from my husband. This confirmed me in the certainty of his death. To make this certainty still more secure, I sought out the messenger, and with a palpitating heart asked him if he had heard any news of my husband in Rome. He had not, nor did he know the name. I informed him he was the captain of the escort of the English Mission. He told me he had seen the captain of the English Mission, but that was not his name; and he then described him, but the description was not my husband's. I made other inquiries, but I found the man had been but a few days in Rome before he was ordered to return to Paris, from whence he had started, and then to continue his journey to London.

I now resolved to remain secluded till the official notice of my lord's death arrived, and then I would put up masses for his soul. I now more frequently saw the Vidame; but although not a word of love passed between us, both too evidently knew the feeling we had for each other. To my shame, this feeling was the more inexcusable on my part, as I had heard from more than one person that the Vidame was a most vicious and dishonest character—hypocritical, selfish, and cowardly: in fact, a reputation the reverse of my dear lord's; but love had closed my eyes to his faults, and in spite of reason I persisted in my blindness.

Another messenger arrived from Rome, and brought a letter from my husband. As soon as I saw his seal and superscription all strength fled from me, and I fell senseless on the ground. My servants carried me to my room and placed me on my bed. Shortly afterwards I somewhat recovered, but it was some hours before I could summon the courage to read the letter. At last I succeeded. In it my lord told me that he had quitted Rome with one of the bishops of the Mission when the last messenger had left, or he should have sent me a letter by him, knowing the happiness it would have given me, (oh! how I blushed when I read that sentence!) He was sorry to say it would be at least three months before the Mission would return, but then he prayed that we might both meet in health and happiness. He, moreover, told me the Holy Father had given him a rosary to present to me, which His Holiness had blessed before the celebration of midnight mass on Christmas Eve, and which my dear husband had attended.

The last part of this letter terrified me. Shortly after that rosary had been blessed by His Holiness for my benefit, the dead, loathsome hand had clasped mine.

Now, for the first time, my dreadful sin appeared to me

A Legend of Wilton Abbey.

in its true light, and I shuddered at my iniquity. I resolved in my heart I would endeavour to repent me of my fault and behave as a dutiful, loving wife. My reason told me I could only do so by breaking my connexion with the Vidame; but how to accomplish it? The hold he had taken on my heart seemed too strong to be renounced. For days I remained trying to frame my mind so as to carry my good resolutions into effect, and I prayed to Heaven to assist me; but my prayers were mere words, there was no earnestness in them.

At last I resolved to drive all love for the Vidame from me, but retain his friendship. I could thus love my husband like a faithful, honest wife, and preserve the society of the Vidame in the position of a friend, and in no other light. The more I reflected on this idea, the more it pleased me. At the same time, I had made no prayer to Heaven for support; on the contrary, I avoided all prayer till my meeting with the Vidame was over.

An opportunity of carrying my resolve into effect at last occurred. It was on a fine evening in the early spring when the Vidame called on me, after I had refused to see him for more than a week, that I might summon up sufficient courage to speak to him calmly on the subject of our acquaintance. The effect of my refusal to see him for so long a time was visible on his handsome countenance. He was pale, very pale, and there was a look of sorrow on his face which went to my heart. But I was determined to adhere to my resolution, and I began the conversation.

"Vidame," I said, "you know my dear husband, before a few months are passed, will return home; and I now wish to speak with you on the subject of our acquaintance—it must cease."

Noticing a look of grief on his countenance, I continued

—" Let not my determination hurt you; but, on reflection, you will see it will be for the happiness of both of us in this world, and our eternal welfare hereafter."

"But why," he said, "insist on my seeing you no more? You can have no cause to blame my behaviour. You know, although my sentiments towards you are such as I cannot express without offending you, I have lately given you no cause of offence; nor will I, if you permit me to visit you."

"Still, such a connexion would be dangerous," I said. "Some day you might again overstep the bounds of prudence, and I will not subject my lord's honour to insult."

"I will never do so, I swear to you. Let me have your friendship, and I ask no more. My own passion shall be silent as the grave; no one shall perceive it. Not a look, not a word shall ever escape me that the most severe could blame. You will render me supremely happy if you will allow me your friendship. Refuse me, and life itself will be insupportable, and I swear to you I will seek refuge in death. More than once my sword has been in my hand to enable me to escape your indifference; and if you refuse me, I swear I will not survive two days your husband's arrival in England."

"But," I said, "if I accord you my acquaintance, how can I be certain you will keep your word and not go beyond it?"

"By my faith as a nobleman, by my faith as a Christian, I swear, not one word of love shall pass my lips, if you will accord me your good feeling."

I looked inquiringly at him to discover the truth. Never was good faith stronger shewn on the face of man than on his.

"Give me one sign," said he, "that you will accord me your friendship, and I shall be supremely happy."

I offered him my hand as a pledge. Before he had taken

it, I drew it back with a loud shriek of terror. The same loathsome, clammy hand had clasped it I had felt at the king's feast. Now there could be no doubt. It was the hand of death. It was still full daylight; and had the hand been of this world, I should have seen it. The same horrible sensation followed it. The same numbness of the arm, the same faint, death-like, nauseous sensation pervaded my whole body. The feeling increased, till I found my strength fail me, and I fell senseless on the ground. The Vidame, now greatly alarmed, called the servants from the house, and they carried me half dead to my chamber.

The next day I did not rise from my bed, so terrible had been the shock I had received. The Vidame, I heard, called to inquire after me; but as I now felt I must have committed some grievous sin, and that I was justly punished by Heaven, I told my French handmaid to thank the Vidame for his courtesy, and also to tell him I wished he would not call on me again, as it displeased me.

The girl told me she did not like to give the message, it was too cruel to treat so gallant a gentleman so severely. Her answer kindled my anger.

"Do not dare to disobey me, or you shall directly leave this house. Understand well the purport of my message before you give it. I will have the Vidame call here no more; and I will dismiss any servant that admits him. That is my fixed resolve; put it to him as civilly as you please, so that he understand it."

The girl seemed to hesitate for a moment, and then suddenly left the room.

The moment I was alone—in fact, the moment after I had explained my order to the girl—a new sensation came over me. The nauseous languor that had oppressed me began rapidly to fade away, and in a few moments I rose from my bed in perfect health, though anxious in mind. I dressed myself quickly, and then knelt humbly before the image of the Virgin in my chamber, and prayed earnestly and ardently that she would advise and protect me. Strange to say, my prayer seemed immediately answered.

I then remembered that I had not confessed for many months, and that I had sinned against God by neglecting it. I determined that I would delay no longer than the morrow. I would have done so that day, but I resolved to pass it in meditation, and calmly to reflect on all the occurrences which had taken place since my last confession, that I might forget nothing.

Presently, after my prayer to the Virgin, my French handmaiden came into my chamber. I looked fixedly at her, almost with astonishment, for the expression of her face seemed altered. The good-humoured frankness of her countenance, which I had hitherto liked, seemed changed, and a false gloss of palpable hypocrisy seemed to cover features indicative of unblushing profligacy and cunning. And yet I could not tell in what her face was changed; yet so it was—she whom I had hitherto regarded with great favour I now looked upon with feelings of intense dislike.

The girl began by telling me how sad the Vidame looked, how anxiously he had inquired after my health; but I would not hear her. I made her no answer, but with an impulsive gesture, which admitted no argument, I motioned to her to leave the room. She seemed astonished, but obeyed me, and her absence seemed a relief to me.

The remainder of the day I passed in prayer and meditation, and in resolving what holy man on the morrow I should choose as a confessor; and at last I decided I would confess me at the Church of St Botolph, Bishopgate, as there officiated in it a priest of great learning and sanctity, who did not know me; for, perhaps wrongly, I had a womanly dislike that any priest of my acquaintance should know how weak I

A Legend of Wilton Abbey. 47

had been. I made inquiry at what hour on the morrow I could attend, so that I might be certain to find him. Having correctly ascertained it, I returned home much easier in my mind.

The next morning, after rising, I prepared my thoughts as I best might for my confession. What I lacked in words in my prayers to the Virgin, I endeavoured to compensate by the earnestness of my application. Afterwards I descended to my day-room, and remained there quietly till one hour before the appointed time for my confession, and I then walked, poorly dressed, and with only one of my men following me, to the church. Here I spent the remainder of my time in prayer, till my turn came to approach the confessional.

I began my confession. Without pride I may avow, never was one more candid poured into the ear of a priest. I omitted nothing that I could possibly remember, and before leaving home I had endeavoured to bring to my mind every circumstance connected with my fault. I told him of the feeling I so guiltily had entertained for the Vidame; the terrible miracle of the dead hand, which had occurred so soon after the Holy Father had given the rosary which he had blessed to my husband as a present for me; my wicked apathy at the idea of the death of my dear lord; my shameful sophistry in pretending I wished only for the friendship of the Vidame when my husband returned home, when as I now felt that in my heart it was his love I wished for; and how a second time the miracle of the dead hand had terrified me. I also mentioned the order I had given that the Vidame should be no more admitted, and the manner that on yesterday morning the Virgin had so graciously lent a kind ear to my prayer.

The priest listened patiently, and evidently with great surprise, to my confession. He made many inquiries, all of which I answered openly and without reservation. He asked what kind of a man my dear lord was, and what offence he had given me that I should have felt no sorrow when I believed him dead?

I described to the priest as well as I could, but still imperfectly, the beauteous, noble man my dear lord was—how he had loved me with all his heart, and did all he could think of to please me in all things. I spoke of his learning, his piety, his love for holy things, and every praise I could think of at the moment, less that I believed he deserved them than I would not hide in my confession my own wicked sin.

The priest inquired whether my wicked affection for the Vidame had ended, and whether I again loved my husband as I formerly loved him?

To the first I most conscientiously answered—Yes. I did not at that moment feel the slightest affection for the Vidame. To the second, with shame and sorrow I admitted I did not. I told the priest, with the tears streaming from my eyes, that I had prayed that my love for my husband might be returned to me, but without effect, and that I was wretched I did not possess it, and that I feared I was accursed of Heaven for my grievous sin.

I wept so bitterly when I said this, and was so overwhelmed with sorrow, that the good priest greatly pitied me, and tried to console me.

"Calm yourself, my dear daughter," he said, "and do not fear but your love for your husband will at last be returned to you. It has been withheld from you as a punishment for your sin; but the mercy of Heaven is boundless, and be assured, with repentance and prayer it will again be restored to you. You are not accursed of Heaven; on the contrary, it has had you in its holy keeping; if not blessed, highly art thou favoured among women. The bounty of Heaven in snatching you from the dreadful sin you were about to commit has been accorded to you in a marvellous manner. The dead hand that clasped yours was the hand of sin in its true state, —loathsome and hideous. To others, Satan would have been allowed to offer it so disguised that its hateful nature would not have been known till too late. The rosary given to your husband by the Holy Father in Rome, and blessed by him so soon before you felt the warning on the night of the king's feast, (which you, neglecting the celebration of the holy midnight mass, had carried into the morning of the day of the Nativity,) is another proof of the mercy of Heaven towards you."

He then questioned me on the necessity of my remaining in London, and whether I could not retire into the country. I told him I was a lady of honour to the queen, but that on account of my late ill health I was persuaded I could get permission to retire with but little difficulty. He then advised me to leave the court immediately, to go down to the castle and remain there till my lord's return, passing the time in the practice of good works, occasional fasting, and frequent prayer. If, he told me, I continued in this discipline, I should, he was persuaded, find my love for my dear husband gradually return to me in proportion as my good deeds increased in number. In conclusion he gave me his blessing, and I left him with a heart far happier than I had known for months.

Before I returned home I went to the palace, and saw the chamberlain of the queen. I told him of my strong desire to be relieved of the duty which had been accorded me in naming me as a lady of honour, but that I felt I was not happy in London, and I prayed his good offices with the queen to be allowed to leave the court. He kindly promised he would carry my wish to her majesty, and support it with his influence, and that he had no doubt he should succeed; and he was right, for the same night I received the royal permission to leave London.

When I arrived at home my first duty was to retire to my room, and there in solitude to thank the blessed Virgin for the protection she had afforded me, and the far happier state of mind I was then in than I had been accustomed to for many months. I afterwards called for my French chamber-maiden. When she came into the room her face displeased me so greatly that I wondered how I could have been blinded to the bad expression she shewed in it. I told her I should no longer require her, and that I would pay her her wages up to the day, and give her a liberal donation beyond, if she left the house within an hour, (for her face was now so hateful to me,) but if she did not, she should only have her wages and nothing beyond. She flauntingly said she would go immediately, as she did not want to stop. She also looked at me most insolently, as if she would willingly have replied to me impertinently; but she said nothing more, possibly from my not yet having given her the money I conditionally promised. Shortly afterwards a man-at-arms told me she was ready, so I sent her the full money I had promised her, and she went away and I never saw her afterwards.

I now gave orders for our departure into the country, to the great joy of our old priest and the men-at-arms. I found all would be ready to start in two days. But before I left London, I received another letter from my dear lord. In it he told me he was in good health, but unfortunately the mission would not return so soon as I had hoped; but that I was not to be down-hearted, as he did not think it would be delayed more than a month longer than he had before stated, but of that he could not be quite sure. But his letter contained still more. As he could not come so soon as he had desired, he had sent me the rosary which had been blessed by the Holy Father on the night of Christmas eve.

I cannot say how delighted I was to receive the rosary, and

with what reverence I took it in my hand. I immediately knelt and went through the beads, and when I rose from my knees I already felt a thrill of love for my noble lord, which gladdened me exceedingly. I then resolved that that blessed rosary should never leave me, and I made preparations to fasten it into my dress, which I did, so that it could not be lost. The day after the receipt of the letter and the rosary all was ready for my departure, and I left London with a willing heart.

CHAPTER V.

WE all arrived safely at the castle without anything worthy to be noted having occurred on the journey. Not only all the old servants appeared delighted to see me, but our tenants and peasantry as well. I visited the latter in turn as soon after my arrival as circumstances would allow me, and assisted those in need, if not to the most in my power, at least as far as they required or merited. I then drew out for myself a line of conduct I considered ought to be pursued by me to carry out the recommendation of the good priest of St Botolph. I divided my time, part in prayer, part in the performance of good works, giving charity not only to the poor, but also in procuring masses for the souls of those of our tenants who had departed this life, and the means of whose friends would not allow them conveniently to carry out the ordinances of our Holy Church in regard to souls in purgatory. I fasted two days in each week, and on each of those days I prayed unceasingly for some hours, that God would forgive me my great sin, and fully restore me to the love I had formerly held for my dear husband. On all these occasions the rosary which had been blessed by our Holy Father at Rome was in my hands, and never did I cease from wearing it.

By degrees, as I practised this system, I found the words of the priest of St Botolph come true, and gradually but perceptibly the love for my dear husband returned to me, and after a short time Heaven, to my great joy, restored it fully to me. Although I had recovered my love for my dear lord, and my repose and security in the mercy of Heaven was great, I did not in anywise cease the discipline ordained me by my confessor, but continued it, especially the performance of good works, to the full of my limited ability. I will not mention all the cases of sickness and distress I visited, as it would appear that I was proud of my exertions, as well as it would not be necessary to this my confession; but I will relate two, as touching on the accomplishment of my present task.

One of the first visits after I had arrived at the castle was to the cottage of my foster sister, Bertha, whom I had dismissed from my service in London. I then imagined her to be excessively impertinent in speaking of the Vidame in the manner she did; but now her behaviour appeared to me in a totally different light, and I already saw that she had been actuated by both love for me and respect for my dear lord. It is true, her language and behaviour had been somewhat upstart and rude, and wanting in the respect due to one her superior; but I reflected that she was not of gentle birth, and I should excuse her rudeness in consideration of the good feeling which had caused it.

Bertha, soon after her return to the castle, married a hind who had land, which he held of my lord, and which was well stocked with cattle. Her husband also was a good, handsome man, a few years older than herself; and they lived very happily together, he being greatly attached to his wife, and Bertha was equally fond of her husband. All this I heard from the people at the castle, who looked upon them with great good feeling, and spoke most highly of them.

It was on a fine afternoon that I paid my first visit to Bertha. As I approached her cottage I was in great trepidation, as I was somewhat doubtful what reception I should meet with—all the other tenants on the estate having called at the castle shortly after my return, but Bertha and her husband had not been among the number. However, I had a duty of humility to perform, and I was determined to accomplish it, though it greatly oppressed me to think I was obliged to ask pardon of a menial. One precaution I had taken, which rendered my task less painful, I had chosen the time for my visit when I knew her husband would be absent in the fields at his daily labour.

When I entered the cottage I found Bertha alone. Her back was towards me, and it gave me a moment's time to recover my self-possession. I called her by her name, and she turned round in a startled manner. When she recognised me she was so surprised she could say nothing, neither could I find words to address her. Bertha was the first to recover herself. She spoke not, but, in a proud and offended manner, drew herself up to her full height, and looked inquiringly in my face as if she would ask why I had called on her. I was the first to speak.

"Bertha," I said, "I have called upon you to ask you to forgive me for treating you in the manner I did when we were in London. I behaved to you harshly and unkindly, and although you expressed yourself somewhat rudely, I am sure you were actuated at the time by a warm love both for me and my dear husband. Will you forgive me, Bertha?"

I cannot tell the great change which came over the girl's face when she heard me. At first, she appeared as if she could not believe me—as if I were speaking to her in mockery—but as she perceived I was perfectly serious, her countenance rapidly changed into an expression of gratitude and love. She tried to speak, but she could say nothing. She then advanced, and still without speaking a word, she cast her arms round my neck, and wept like a child. Nor was my joy much less than hers; I pressed her to my heart, and felt so happy, that I could not restrain myself, but wept as foolishly as Bertha herself.

When we had a little recovered ourselves, we soon found the use of our tongues, and were no longer silent. We conversed about my husband's return; and I shewed her the rosary which he had sent me, and which had been blessed by our Holy Father the Pope. Bertha asked permission to take it in her hand; and to please her, I loosened it, with some difficulty, from my dress. When she had taken it from me, she kissed it reverently, and then prayed by it. She then returned it to me, saying, that I was happy to have so holy a treasure. I next inquired into her present welfare and future prospects, and was well pleased to hear the report of her worldly possessions which I had heard of had not been overrated, but were rather more flourishing than I had imagined. I listened to all with pleasure; and I believe I felt as much satisfaction in hearing of her happiness as she had in narrating it. Not one word, however, passed between us about anything which had taken place during our residence in London—in fact, if neither had been there, nor knew of its existence, it could not have been more perfectly omitted from our conversation.

I learned, however, that great as was Bertha's happiness, it was not without alloy. A sister, about a year older than herself, had married a man who had been obliged to leave her to accompany my lord to Rome. A few months after his departure, his wife was confined. The child was, to the great joy of its mother, a boy; but, on the other hand, it was sickly and not likely to survive. Nevertheless, it lived on and was the great delight of the poor woman during the absence of her husband. But not only was the delicate constitution of her child a source of anxiety to her, but a personal affliction befell her as well. A disease of the knee attacked her, and as her own health was not good, and as the constant attention her infant required fatigued her greatly, she was soon thrown on a bed of sickness.

As Bertha herself had no prospect of a family, which she sorely regretted, she took even more than the natural interest an affectionate sister would feel for the welfare of the poor child, and it appeared to be a considerable portion of her daily duties to walk over to her sister's cottage and assist her in her misfortunes to the best in her power. She discoursed to me for a long time on the subject, asking me many questions which I could not answer, and requesting my advice upon many things which I did not understand.

I asked Bertha how far off her sister lived, and she told me that it was not more than a mile, and that it was even nearer to the castle than her own cottage. I immediately offered to visit her sister, if she would go with me, to shew me the way. I shall not easily forget the girl's look of gratitude when I made her the offer. She thanked me for my condescension, (for she had for some time regained possession of herself, and now treated me with proper respect as well as affection,) and said she would willingly go with me if I had no objection to walk with her.

She then went to prepare herself for her walk, while I in the meantime looked around her cottage to see if there was anything she needed that I could give her without letting her know of my intention. But I could discover nothing necessary for her condition in life that she did not possess—a fact which hardly gave me satisfaction, as I had determined in my mind to make her some present which might be of use to her. I, however, determined that I would give her a handsome gown for Sundays and feast days, which I afterwards did to her great satisfaction, for Bertha was very pretty, and liked dress perhaps too much.

In a few moments Bertha was ready, and we left the house. On our road to her sister's, I discovered that she was much poorer than Bertha, and often wanted many things which were necessary for her unfortunate position. Even more, that had it not been for the liberality of Bertha's husband, who had been very generous to the poor creature, as well as the affectionate care of Bertha herself, she possibly might have died from want. In one respect I was not sorry to hear this, as it pointed out to me a manner in which I might be able to do good, and I had already resolved not to miss such an opportunity. I told Bertha I would willingly assist her sister in all things I could, and moreover requested her to tell me how I could benefit the unfortunate woman, as I would help her if I knew the way.

Bertha again thanked me gratefully for my kindness. She told me she feared, great as my generosity might be, that should not be able to assist her in the most material point. What her sister most needed was a skilful leech, and there was none in those parts. The best they had was an old woman, and she worked generally by spells. Moreover, there was a very great suspicion that she was an emissary of Satan, and worked by his agency. She also mentioned several cases where the old woman had attended good pious persons, without their receiving any advantage therefrom, and other cases where the patients were persons of indifferent reputation, who recovered from their complaints, but that afterwards either some sore misfortunes befell them, or they were taken for some grievous crime, and either imprisoned or hanged, which also went to shew that she worked with the power of the Evil One, who was always paid by a sin for every assistance he gave.

I told her there was no doubt she was right; and I advised her to employ the old woman no more, as the fact of her having been powerless on the good, proved her to be in connexion with the Evil One. Bertha was much pleased to find that my opinion corresponded with hers, as with my superior knowledge to support her, she would advise her sister no longer to see the old woman, although it was a hard case, seeing no other help was at hand. But in this I consoled her by telling her that a new priest had come to live at the castle, (the old one was now bedridden,) who had great skill in medicine, and that he should visit her sister, and assist her both with his spiritual consolation and his knowledge of healing as well. In conversation such as this the time passed quickly, and I did not feel the fatigue the walk to the sick woman's house would otherwise have occasioned me.

When we arrived, I found Bertha's sister even more to be pitied than I had anticipated. From the inflammation in her knee, she was unable to leave her bed, yet her sick baby required incessant attention. I also noticed that the furniture and means of her cottage were very poor and defective; but this did not give me so much pain as it otherwise would have done had I not had it in my power to assist her, not only in finding requisites, but comforts as well. She seemed much pleased with my visit, and more so when I asked to see her baby, which I praised very much, and said it was very pretty, though at the same time my heart bled to see how thin and weak it was. So sickly was it, that when I took it in my arms and fondled it to please her, I was thankful when I had restored it to her, for I almost feared the movement was too much for its little strength.

Before I left her, I inquired what things she was most in need of, as I would send them to her. I also told her not to let the wicked old woman visit her again, as I was sure she was a witch, and that if the baby through her means recovered its strength, (which I did not believe, for it was so weak it seemed nearly dead,) it would not advantage it, for if she received her help from Satan, which I really believed she did, the child when it grew up would be wicked and come to some bad end, or be attacked by some cruel malady and never recover. I also told her the new priest who was learned in medicine should attend her, and that she should want for nothing I could furnish her with. I shortly afterwards left them to return home with my serving-man, who had accompanied me to both houses, but who had watched outside the while.

When I arrived at home that day, I felt so happy that I thanked God for His great goodness in restoring me to my peace of mind. I also found my love for my dear husband had returned to me, for in the evening a messenger brought me a letter from him, and the joy I felt at its contents fully proved he was now as dear to me as ever. In it he told me that in a few days they were to leave Rome and proceed to London; but that they would be obliged to remain three or four days in Paris. As soon as the affairs which obliged their resting in that city were over, he would hurry on to England; and he sincerely hoped and believed, that a week after I had received the letter he would be with me again.

The inexpressible joy this intelligence gave me made me act as some one almost demented. I laughed and cried without reason, and could not collect my thoughts together for a moment at a time, so that I might give orders to send the things I had promised to Bertha's sister. When, at last, I had recovered my presence of mind, I found that Bertha herself had followed me home to take back to her sister some linen I had promised her. When I heard her voice, (for she was in another room when I first found she was in the castle,) I rushed to her and told her the joyful intelligence I had received. She looked at me inquiringly for a moment, and then with great satisfaction in her countenance congratulated me on my happiness. She also said, it grieved her that her poor sister's husband should find her so ill, and the baby in so dangerous a condition. I said, it was certainly very sad, and that I was very sorry for it; but, in truth, the state of contentment I was in made me selfish, and I thought but little of the poor woman.

Bertha's presence, however, after a short time recalled me to the purport of her visit, and I immediately sent for the priest, who attended me directly. I told him quickly what I wished him to do; that he was to return to the sick woman's cottage with Bertha, and they were to take with them what things would be likely to be immediately wanted; also, that he was to make a list of everything that would be required, as it was my wish the poor creature should want for nothing; and that the next morning he should wait on me and let me know what he would advise should be done in the case, so that no time (it was then evening) should be lost.

I slept but little that night. More than once I rose from my bed, and on my knees humbly thanked God and the blessed Virgin for having restored me again to a happy frame of mind. I then thought of my dear lord; how pleased he would be when he saw me again, and how many questions I would ask him of how he had spent his time in Rome, and what sort of people the Romans were, and many other things which it would be tedious to mention. I once thought on the great sin I had committed, and the greater from which Heaven in its mercy had snatched me, and whether I ought to inform my lord of any part, or all, of my faults; but my mind was soon at ease on that point. I resolved that I would take an opportunity of again confessing to the holy priest of Saint Botolph, and there on my knees request his guidance and advice, resolutely determining to abide by it, whatever it might be, even to declaring to my dear lord in everything what a sinner I had been. I had received so much strength and consolation from the last confession I had made, I had no fear for the result of the next.

When I arose the next morning, my first thought was to thank God that He had brought me one day nearer to my dear husband's return, and this I did with a most grateful and devout heart. After my breakfast the priest presented himself to me to give an account of his visit to Bertha's sister. He told me the child was sick unto death, and that he feared he should be hardly able to save it, and that he attributed its exhausted condition to the ignorance or malpractice of the old woman who had attended it. From all he could learn, he believed that she had used unholy appliances, taught her by Satan, but that he would not judge too harshly of her till he had seen the effect of his medicine both upon the mother and child, the former of whom he considered also to be very sick, but not in such danger as the infant. He told me, in the first place, that both mother and child wanted good nourishment, and for that end they ought to have the best milk for their porridge that could be found. He would, therefore, ask that a red cow from the herd should be sent to the cottage, as cows of that colour gave far stronger milk than any others. Further, that I would send many fowls for his use, not as food but as medicaments. Some he would require to be killed for the mother, and as soon as dead, or before, to be cut open to be applied to her knee. Others he wanted for the infant, as the inner skin of a hen's maw, dried and mixed with a certain drug he had, which had been brought from the East by pilgrims, but the name of which I now forget, was excellent for all weakly children. He also asked for a newly tanned hide, fresh from the tan-yard, on which he would lay the child naked, that the strength of the hide might communicate itself to the child, and increase its strength thereby.

All these requests I immediately complied with, and I was grateful to Providence who had sent to the poor so learned a man to assist them in their need, and I thought it fortunate that the child was no longer in the power of the ignorant old woman. I further told the priest that towards evening I would also visit Bertha's sister, and I then hoped to find that his ministrations had been used with good effect.

In the evening I kept my word, and went to the sick woman's cottage. I found the poor mother very grateful for the kindness I had shewn her, but as yet they had not been able to reap any benefit therefrom, as the time had been so short. The baby was much worse than it had been the day before; indeed, I could notice a great change, which was not perceptible to the mother. Moreover, the medicine the priest had given it would in no way stay upon its stomach, notwithstanding that he had often put it into its mouth. He told me he thought the old woman had bewitched it, and that was the reason his medicine had no better effect. I thought so too, but I forebore to pass any judgment on the old woman, as I did not think so great a sinner as I had been should sit in judgment on another perhaps not more wicked than myself.

CHAPTER VI.

WHEN I arose next morning I twice went through my beads, in gratitude to God that He had brought me another day nearer to my dear husband. I did not leave the castle that morning, for the weather was very stormy. I waited till the afternoon, hoping it would then be fine enough to allow me to visit the poor sick woman; but as the rain still poured down, and the wind was more boisterous than ever, I sent a serving man to inquire whether the woman and her baby were in better health, and whether they were in want of anything I could send them.

In about two hours' time the man came back again with very mournful intelligence. He told me that Bertha's sister might be better in health, but that her grief at the state her infant was in was so great as not to allow the progress of her own cure to be apparent. That the priest, who had been with the sick woman all day, told him to say he thought it almost impossible that the baby could live the night through, so much had its health been injured by the old woman's malpractices who had attended it before his arrival. The only hope for the poor infant now was in the power of Heaven, (which was omnipotent,) to snatch it from the grave, and that he wished, and that Bertha prayed, I would lend them my rosary, which had been blessed by the Holy Father at Rome, that they might put it round the child, and thus possibly save its life.

As I had made a vow my rosary should never leave me,

and as I would on no account leave the child's health a moment in doubt if I had the power to help it, I had no alternative but to brave the storm and visit the house of the poor woman myself. I ordered my horse immediately to be got ready for me, and as soon as it was brought to the door I mounted it. My serving-man led it for me, as I was obliged to hold tightly my mantle around me, so fierce was the storm. Indeed, even then, I had some difficulty to prevent being thrown down, so strong was the wind. The serving-man also carried with him a torch to light, in case it should be dark when we returned home.

We at last, though with some difficulty, arrived at the cottage, and within it there was indeed a sad sight. The poor woman was seated in her bed, with her infant on her lap. She was trying to claim its attention by saying what pretty little words she could to it, but without success. She would smile at it, and with her mild, gentle voice call it her own dear one, her sweet and her pretty, but the while she spoke and smiled, and moved her head to it, the big tears ran down her own cheeks, for the infant gave no sign of notice, but gazed with a dull, leaden look at her face, as if it knew it not.

I had been some moments in the cottage before they were aware of my presence; they were all so occupied with the child, Bertha being on her knees beside the bed, trying to prepare some food for it, which, alas! it was easy to perceive it was impossible for it to take, and the priest had his back to me mixing some medicine, which I could also easily perceive it had not the strength to swallow. When they recognised me a change immediately came over the whole, and so pleased did they appear to see me, that had I been an angel (I speak with all humility) they could hardly have been more joyful. But, alas! I was but a poor mortal like themselves, and perhaps a greater sinner than either, and could not help them beyond lending them my rosary.

But in a short time I was as sad as the rest, for the poor mother, when she saw me, left her baby in her lap, and taking hold of both my hands in hers, she pressed her lips upon them, and bathed them with her tears. She implored me to save her baby, if only till her dear husband returned with my lord, but, alas! as I said before, I could not help her beyond lending my rosary and giving her my prayers.

The priest then came to the bed, and I detached my rosary from my side. He first crossed himself, and then, taking it from me, he placed it round the neck of the baby, at the same time putting a portion of the tanned hide beneath it. We then prayed that the baby might receive strength from it, if it was Heaven's good will, and if not, that we might have humble hearts to bear the infliction, and that God and the Blessed Virgin would comfort the poor mother in her trouble, and prepare the heart of her husband to submit with resignation to his loss.

But though our prayers were doubtless heard, Heaven in its wisdom did not accord us the boon we asked for. The infant got gradually worse, but the blessed rosary was not without its good effects, for the pain the poor baby had hitherto been suffering suddenly ceased, and it breathed on easily and quietly for perhaps two hours, when it died.

As its spirit left us, we all prayed silently, but so earnestly that I do not think one of us heard the storm which raged without. When our prayer was ended, we rose from our knees, and I seated myself on the edge of the bed and tried to console the poor mother for her loss with what little ability I had, while the priest took the body of the child and laid it decently on a stool, and placed a candle at its head, which also lighted the room, for it was already dark. He also returned me my rosary, and told the poor mother that it was a happy thing for her baby's soul that the rosary was round it when it died;

to which she bowed her head, as if in token of the truth of his statement, but with little consolation to her grief.

I remained with the poor woman for more than two hours after the death of her child, and then, as the night was far advanced, I sent for my serving-man, and told him to prepare my horse and light his torch, that we might proceed homewards. When he was ready I took a long leave of them all, (for I requested the priest to remain and comfort the poor woman,) and then, with the help of my serving-man, I mounted my horse. The night was intensely dark, and the storm raged so furiously that I wondered, with all our grief, we had not heard it more plainly in the cottage. We proceeded but slowly, as the man had great difficulty in keeping his torch alight, and leading the horse at the same time.

After we had left the cottage about a quarter of an hour, a sudden gust of wind blew out the torch. We tried to continue our road without it, but the night was so dark, and the horse stumbled so frequently, we found it would be impossible, so I told the serving-man to place me in shelter under some trees, where I could remain in safety while he returned to the cottage to relight his torch. He then helped me from my horse, which he fastened to the stump of some bushes as well as he could, and placed me a short distance from it under some trees. He afterwards left me to seek the cottage, where he might again obtain a light.

After the man had left me I felt in my solitude no fear, but great sadness. While we were in motion, the task of finding the way, as well as the difficulty in avoiding danger, kept my mind fully occupied; but now that excitement was wanting, my thoughts reverted to the sad scene which had occurred in the cottage. I had never before seen death, and the sight of the dead body of the infant, as it lay stretched on the stool by the priest, with the candle burning at its head, filled my mind with a sensation of holy awe. I thought in how short a time was the soul of the poor baby transferred from the sins and sorrows of the world to rise to an eternity of bliss in another. But while I admired the bounty of Heaven in taking the poor infant to itself, I lamented the misery of the mother now childless, and the sorrowful meeting which would take place between her and her husband on his return. I compared their affliction to my own joy when my dear lord should arrive, and the comparison, without lessening my pity for the unhappy couple, added a prayer of gratitude to Heaven on my part for the great bliss I should enjoy.

My prayer finished, I remained for some time marking the strength of the terrible storm that was then raging. It appeared to increase rather than diminish, and the howling of the wind was fearful. It blew so strongly that the trees bent and quivered under its force, and more than once the cracking noise of the branches, as they were broken from the trunk, filled me with terror, though, fortunately, none fell very near the tree under which I was standing. Still it alarmed me, and I wished to move from the spot I stood on for one more open, being willing rather to expose myself to the rudeness of the elements than run the danger of perhaps some heavy-falling bough which might be torn by the storm from the trunk under which I was standing. I had not, however, the courage to move; why I knew not, for I am not generally easily alarmed. I endeavoured to bring my thoughts back to the cottage, and I began to consider in what way I could help the poor bereaved mother in her sorrow, and I determined I would visit her again the next morning, and console her as I best could, and assist her in other ways to the utmost in my power.

I then thought I had done well in leaving the priest with her, and how great the consolation he would be able to give her, when the falling of a large branch near me startled me so much that I trembled like an aspen leaf. I still felt unable to move. I bethought me to commend my soul to Heaven, and my hand sought my rosary, As the beads passed through my fingers I found myself more at peace; still a strong feeling of sad oppression was over me, though the fear had left me.

I now bent forward my head to see if my serving-man was coming, and I looked down the pathway, but all was pitchy dark; there was no sign of him. I then got impatient and somewhat angry with him for what appeared to me his great delay, but now I believe I did the man an injustice, and that it was only my own unreasonable impatience which caused the feeling.

Presently another change took place in my mind. I seemed to feel a dull chilling sort of apathy. I shuddered at the cold, but felt I cared not for it. In this state I remained for some moments, when I was called to my right senses by a terrible blast of wind which swept through the trees. I now thought of my dear lord, and how rude such weather was for him to travel in, and I hoped he had escaped it. I then began to feel most anxious about him, but my anxiety gradually subsided, and I listened to the howling of the terrible storm. Presently I began to listen more attentively, for it appeared to me to change in its sound. A noise of rushing water seemed mixed with it, far greater than even the great rain which had fallen would warrant.

I then bethought me of a brook which I knew ran somewhere near the spot I was standing on, and for a moment I dwelt no more on the rushing of the water; but presently the same sound again rose on the ear, but far louder and more distinct than before. It increased till I could perfectly recognise the loud dashing of water upon rocks, and the hissing noise the spray would make as it leapt from them in the air. I next remembered the noises of the sea in the stormy night which followed my lord's departure from England, and which I clearly heard in my chamber in Dover Castle, though now the roar was far louder and more distinct. At last I became so terrified I thought I should have fallen, when a fearful alarm gave me a moment's strength. A few paces from me a noble tree was torn from its roots, and with an awful crash it fell to the ground, carrying with it the branches of the trees amidst which it fell.

My alarm at the first moment was so great that it deprived me of the power of movement. I gazed with terror at the fallen gigantic tree, and yet I felt almost pity at its fate. I then turned from it to move farther away, but I advanced not a step. I stood like a statue, motionless with surprise and awe. In turning to move from the spot, I saw near me, distinctly and positively as in broad daylight, the face of my dear lord. So distinct was it that I could perfectly trace every feature in it. It wore exactly the same sweet expression of sorrow and love it bore when last I saw him as the boat moved from the shore when he left England. In no way was it changed. I remembered too well the sad glance he there gave me to be mistaken. As soon as my gaze rested upon it, it disappeared. It was not before me for more than a moment, but it is now as fresh on my mind as at the time I saw it.

I cannot properly describe the sensation which now came over me. It was an overwhelming awe without one particle of terror mixed with it. Though it seemed to cast a sensation of tranquillity on my mind, it weighed on my frame so oppressively that I sank gradually on the ground. I there remained on my knees motionless, my hands clasped as if in prayer, and yet I prayed not. I seemed to feel the sensation of some holy spirit being near me, of whose existence I was perfectly aware without being able to identify its form or position. How long I remained thus I know not, but I was awakened to the realities of life by my serving-man calling to me in a terrified tone of voice. He had arrived at the tree which had fallen across the path, and feared it might have injured me. I attempted to answer him, but it was some moments before I succeeded, and then in a tone of voice so faint and inarticulate, he thought some misfortune had befallen me. He climbed with his lighted torch with some difficulty over the tree, and approached the spot on which I knelt. He attempted to raise me, but I could not stand, so he brought the horse to me, and at last contrived to place me more dead than alive on its back.

We now proceeded homewards. Although my serving-man asked me if I was hurt, and although I wished to answer him, as he appeared alarmed at my condition, it was so painful to me to talk that I said nothing. In a short time we emerged from the wood and got into the open country, and our way was easier to find. We now advanced more rapidly, and presently I began to distinguish the lights in the castle windows, which gave me some spirit; still I was sad, awe-struck, and silent. When we arrived near to the entrance-gates the porter, as well as the other servants, advanced to meet me, and overwhelmed me with congratulations at my safe arrival, and inquiries as to the manner I had braved the storm, to all of which I would give but little answer, and that almost inaudible. Finding me so silent, and fearing I was ill, an old nurse advised me to go straight-way to bed, which, with her assistance, I immediately did. But even there neither sleep nor comfort would come to me, and I remained the greater part of the night in a state of torpor I could not arouse from.

The next morning was calm and bright, and formed a strange contrast with the storm of the evening before. I attempted to pray, yet hardly succeeded, although the while I had the blessed rosary in my hand; and yet I felt no sensation of Heaven's anger on me for any sin I might have committed, but rather the contrary; a degree of calm even more than I had been lately used to. Nevertheless, I carefully examined my conscience, but without finding I had committed any great sin more than is liable to mortals, which I had not accounted for.

After breakfast I walked alone to the poor woman's house. On the road thither the calm, fine morning acted soothingly upon me, and my mind became clearer. Presently I arrived at the spot where the great tree had fallen the evening before. When I saw the huge mass lying on the ground, and marked the ruin it had caused on the trees near it, many of which had been sorely damaged by its fall, I thanked God with a humble and grateful heart for all His mercies, and especially for having spared me the last night, so that I might live to praise Him, and, in second degree, to meet again my noble lord.

After having marked the spot where I had seen the vision of my dear husband the evening before, and noticed how close it was to the fallen tree, I again went on my way. As I walked quietly along I bethought me what the apparition of my lord's countenance to me the night before should mean. I could not in any way make it clear to my mind; the only idea which presented itself to me was that my dear lord was in spirit always near me, and that it was for his virtues that I was spared the night before, and that the vision was kindly sent me as a proof.

I confess this reasoning did not clearly satisfy me, but I could find no better. At one time I thought I would consult the new priest on the subject, but I was restrained by a womanly, though perhaps a wrong feeling. I knew but little of him beyond that he had great skill in curing wounds and diseases, and I did not like, on so short an acquaintance, to converse with him on affairs connected with my lord and myself.

Before I had arrived at the cottage I heard a great noise of shouting to my left hand. At first I paid little attention to it, not being in a humour to interest myself in what did not concern me; but presently I heard violent shrieks, as if from a female voice in great terror. I rested for a moment and listened more attentively. No, I was not deceived, it was certainly the scream of some woman in mortal fear, for, loud as the shouts were, her voice rose above them.

I immediately went to the spot from whence the noise proceeded, and there found a crowd of men, perhaps twenty, with some women. They appeared highly excited, and were dragging along with them towards a pond an old woman, who was still screaming violently while they hurried her along, abusing her and cursing her the while. When they saw me they stopped, and one of their number, a man, came forward and respectfully told me they had caught the old witch at last, and they were going to drown her, as they were determined she should do no more mischief.

Without answering him, I advanced to the riotous mob, who opened and made way for me, and I thus saw plainly the witch whom they would kill. She was an old ill-favoured woman, dressed in rags, and presented a sad spectacle, for her face was covered with her tears and dirt, and her loose gray hair hung down over her shoulders. When she saw me she rushed towards me; flinging herself on the ground at my feet, and taking the hem of my robe she kissed it, and begged of me, as a great lady, to protect her.

I said to her, "Thou wicked woman, what hast thou done?"

She answered me that she had done nothing wrong; that she was a poor old woman oppressed by all, and without cause.

All the men and women present here, with one voice, said it was not true; that she was a wicked witch, and had great power with the evil one; that by her devilish sorceries she had not only killed the baby of Bertha's sister with such powerful spells that even the prayers and medicines of the holy priest, who afterwards attended it, had no power against them, and that she had, by the aid of the Prince of Darkness, raised the terrible storm which yesterday evening had passed over the land, destroying the crops and casting desolation on all the country around.

The old woman here, calling on the Virgin and all the saints, swore most solemnly the men were wrong, that she had no power to do harm more than was in her own hands, and that could not be much, as they were now too feeble to till the little garden which had hitherto given her food.

I asked the men what proof they had that the old woman was a witch, as it was a very wicked thing to persecute her if they had none.

They said they had good and sufficient proof that the old woman was a wicked witch, not only in respect to the poor infant which she had killed, but in relation to the storm itself. While it was at its height a number of hinds collected together, and wondered what such a terrible storm, the like of which for many years had not passsed over the land, might mean. They then spoke of the death of the poor baby, for they were all much interested in Bertha's sister, and what had caused it. One among them said he was certain it was done by witchcraft, and that it was a shame that such a wicked old woman as the witch should be allowed to live among them, and that he had no doubt it was she who had raised the terrible storm. Then all said they were also certain she had raised the storm, and that she ought to die. At last they agreed they would drown her on the morrow, but no sooner had they come to their decision than, to their great wonder, the storm began to abate, and gradually in a short time it ceased altogether.

I was obliged to admit in my own mind that the proof seemed conclusive, but at the same time the poor wretched creature, crouching at my feet in abject terror, excited my pity greatly. I reflected for a moment what answer I would make. In a ltttle time it occurred to me that the amount of mischief which had been done by the storm was too vast to be accomplished by an old woman, and that even the casting down the huge tree which had nearly crushed me was impossible for her with her weak hands to do, even with the aid of a fiend to counsel her; and that if the hinds were wrong in that, they might be equally in error as to the cause of the baby's death. Still, I was obliged to admit the proof they brought forward told terribly against her.

At last I determined I would send to the sick woman's cottage, and if the priest were still there I would beg him to attend me immediately to give me his advice in a matter of great difficulty.

Fortunately he was in the cottage, and he immediately waited on me. When he saw the old woman he crossed himself, and advised me not to let her hold the hem of my robe. I would willingly have obeyed him but I had not the heart, so much had the wretched creature interested me in her cause, so I crossed myself and then took my rosary in my hand, knowing it could protect me from all harm which it was not Heaven's will should befall me. Even the priest seemed secure when he saw what I did, and did not repeat his advice.

But no sooner had I taken the rosary in my hand than through it and Heaven's influence a thought occurred to me, (it must have been through its influence, tor the thought was just, wise, and merciful,)—it was to make the old woman take the rosary in her hand, and then to call on God and all the saints that she had committed no sorcery, neither in the

A Legend of Wilton Abbey.

case of Bertha's sister's baby, nor the storm of last evening, nor in any other case. Also, that if she swore falsely that she hoped she might either be struck dead, or that Heaven would condescend to give some immediate token that they might be aware of her guilt.

I took the priest aside and told him my plan. He said he thought the proof was a good one, as it would be impossible for her, if she were a witch, to take so terrible an oath with so holy a rosary in her hand, and that furthermore it would give him great joy if she escaped; for although he was certain she had caused the death of the child, it might have been from her ignorance and not her malice, although he greatly feared the contrary.

I was much pleased at his so fully entering into my views. I placed the rosary in his hand, and requested him to administer to her the oath. He willingly assented, and we again joined the crowd, who had in no way injured the old woman during our absence. The priest, first moving the crowd from the terrified creature, asked her in a whisper if she were willing to take the oath in the manner I proposed; to which she gave a most ready and earnest assent. Finding her willing to take the oath, he then made the men and women form a circle round us, and in the centre he placed the old woman on her knees. He again asked her, but aloud this time, if she were willing to submit to the ordeal; to which she again gave her ready answer. He then requested we would all kneel, and he was immediately obeyed. Taking the blessed rosary in his hand he now began to pray aloud.

He humbly called upon Heaven, in its justice, to aid us in our judgment, that we might not err. That our wish was to punish her as an enemy to God if she should prove guilty, or to release her if innocent or ignorant from a wrongful suspicion. He therefore earnestly prayed that Heaven would vouchsafe some sign of its wrath should a punishment be merited, or one of its favour should she be innocent.

He then approached the old woman with the rosary in his hand. He told her to take it in her own, and repeat after him, slowly and distinctly, the words he should utter. He emphatically and solemnly dictated to her the form, making her assert her innocence before Heaven, and calling its utmost vengeance on her head should she by sorcery, directly or indirectly, have been guilty either of the death of the child, or caused the storm of the night before, or have even combined knowingly with Satan, by any unlawful charms or spells, to work injury to any one either in soul or body. He told her when she had concluded to kiss the rosary. The poor woman exactly and with a clear voice repeated the words as he uttered them, and when she had concluded she devoutly kissed the rosary.

For some moments all were silent as the grave, expecting with awe some especial sign of Heaven's anger, for we all in our hearts believed the old woman to be a wicked witch, who had done much mischief in the country, but none came. The morning, which had been bright and calm, appeared to me to become even more so, and as I watched the old woman's face I thought I saw in it, disordered as it was, an expression of innocence I had in no way noticed before. We continued silent for some minutes longer even than when I had fully made up my mind she was not guilty, but nothing occurred to lead her worst enemy to believe she was not innocent. At last the priest was satisfied, and he took from her hand the rosary, and told her to rise, as he was assured of her innocence; and he hoped that all the bystanders, after they had witnessed the appeal which had been made to Heaven, and the marked manner that any manifest token of its displeasnre was withheld, would consider her innocent likewise. Almost all readily promised they would, but two or three still seemed very sullen; but they were people of no account, and nothing was to be feared from them.

The priest then returned me my rosary, but before separating from the old woman he called her to him and told her, that although he was assured of her innocence from all witchcraft, he was still much displeased with her for ignorantly attempting the art of healing, of which she knew nothing; and he further told her, if he found her again meddling with the sick, he would assuredly get her severely punished.

"But what am I to do?" replied the old woman; "I am too weak to labour, and if I do not heal the sick I cannot live."

"I should be sorry," said the priest, "to do you harm; but you have no skill in healing, and shall not practise it."

I said nothing, lest I should be thought to wish to be praised for my goodness, but I determined in my mind she should not starve, and that I would send her both food and raiment, which I did;—but enough of this.

I now walked with the priest to the sick woman's cottage. We did not talk, for my mind was occupied with the wondrous manner the poor old woman had been saved from what appeared a certain death, and I thanked Heaven in my mind for the blessed rosary which I possessed, and which had last night probably saved my own life, and had this morning snatched from the grave a helpless fellow-creature.

When I arrived at the cottage, I found with pleasure that the poor woman was more resigned to her loss than I had anticipated. All this, I believe, was due to the kind teaching and prayers of the priest, who had not left her for a longer time together than would enable him to celebrate the mass at a neighbouring chapel. I found, also, that the infant had been placed in its coffin, and that it had been determined that the funeral should take place the next day, as there was but one room in the cottage, and the priest justly thought that it would be better it should be buried as soon as possible.

I now sat down on the edge of the bed and conversed with the poor woman. She abundantly opened her heart to me, and told me the two sorrows that now oppressed her the most were the grief her husband would experience when he returned at finding the child dead, and the distress she should feel the next day at not being able to attend the funeral in consequence of the inflamed state of her knee. To this I answered, that it was indeed sad, but that, with respect to the funeral, I would myself attend it as chief mourner, and that I would provide both her and her sister with a piece of black cloth to make them each a mourning dress, which Bertha, who was expert with her needle, could make up.

For the last she thanked me, for the former she did more. She took my hand and kissed it, and said that it was too great an honour for them that a lady, the wife of a lord, should follow their child to the grave, and that she was sure my condescension would go far to soothe the grief of her husband on his return. After a little more conversation, I left her in much better heart than she had been in for some days past.

The next day I attended the funeral as I had promised. A boy went first with the cross, and after him the priest in his canonicals, and then a man carrying the poor baby. I then followed as chief mourner, and Bertha walked beside me. Many others were also in the train, but I know not their number. I was glad to find the peasants were pleased at my presence, for they took it very kindly of me, and spoke to each other of my condescension; but of which I thought nothing, for I was too glad to do them a pleasure. When the funeral was over, I returned with Bertha to the cottage.

I remained some hours with Bertha and her sister, and was much pleased to find the latter supported her misfortune more resignedly than I had anticipated. She saw clearly that the poor baby, now in heaven with the blessed, would have been, had it remained with her, in continual pain and danger, and even if it had lived till it was a man, it would most likely have been weak and sickly.

In this manner we conversed together till the evening, when a female neighbour came in; so I then determined to go home, as I wished to take Bertha with me; and the sick woman could, in the meantime, have the company of her neighbour. The walk home was very pleasant—the evening was so calm and beautiful. I had taken Bertha with me, as I wished to send some things back by her to her sister, and also a little food to the old woman whom the hinds had so nearly killed. We conversed together as we walked along, and I shewed Bertha the huge tree which had fallen and nearly crushed me, and I told her I was certain it was my rosary which had saved me; upon which Bertha crossed herself, and said I was a happy lady to have so great a treasure. I was greatly tempted also to tell her of my lord's apparition to me, and the sound of the sea-waves which I had heard; but I remembered that, although a good girl, she was unlearned and timorous; and as she would have to pass the spot on her return home, I thought it might frighten her: so I held my peace.

We then conversed about the speedy arrival in England of my lord and her sister's husband. Bertha said it was a sad thing for her brother-in-law to arrive in England and find his child dead; but I attempted to prove to her that it was better for the baby that it should be in paradise than suffering on earth, and that I had no doubt its father would soon see it in the same light, and other reasonings of the like kind. At the same time, I could not help comparing the sorrow the poor couple would feel when they met with the unmixed joy which awaited my dear lord and myself.

When we approached the castle, I saw many of our people at the gate, and they appeared in a state of great and joyful excitement. When they saw me they came to meet me, the porter at their head. They told me, with great pleasure in their faces, that a messenger had arrived with a letter from London, which, they believed, was from my lord, but of that they were not sure, as the man knew nothing of its contents, nor whom it was from, as he had only been entrusted by another messenger to bring it to me. I inquired where the man was. They said he was in the hall, where they had given him some food, as he had ridden hard, and was greatly fatigued, and in need of refreshment.

I know not the reason, but instead of feeling the joy natural to the occasion, a heavy sensation of dread came over me. I looked in the countenances of those around me, and marked the pleasure on them; but it did not communicate itself to me. Presently their expression of pleasure passed away, and one of surprise and anxiety supplied its place, as they looked earnestly at me. This recalled me to the situation; and I walked forwards towards the hall, but I felt my limbs tremble as I went. When I approached the messenger he rose from the table at which he was seated, and taking from his wallet a letter, he presented it to me. With the letter in my hand, I looked hard at the man, as if I feared the news he brought, and would question him on it before I broke the seal; but he stood my gaze indifferently. I asked him from whom the letter might be. He told me, as I had heard before, that he neither knew the contents nor whom it was from. It had been given to him by a king's messenger in London, with orders to bring it to me as quickly as he might be able.

I now looked at the letter with a sort of dread I could not

account for, and my heart beat so violently, it might almost have been heard. The letter gave from its outside no token whom it might have come from; but the seal, which was large, I noticed was not my lord's, but apparently from some officer of the king's: for the royal crown was on it. I gave a sigh of almost relief, but still I felt anxious. I attempted to untie the string that bound it, but as I could not succeed, Bertha offered me her knife, which I would not take, but used my own bodkin to unloosen the knot, as if I wished to put off knowing the contents of the letter for as long a time as possible.

When I had opened it, I did not know the handwriting, but found it had been sent to me by the governor of Dover Castle. It told me that about mid-day, a few days before, the mission of which my husband commanded the men-at-arms, left in a good ship the harbour of Calais. The weather was then very stormy, and the seamen thought it would be worse, and advised that the mission should delay its departure till the next day, but my lord (there being no bishops with them now, they having remained in Paris) being desirous to arrive in England, gave orders they should weigh the anchor at once. As he was now the chief, they could not disobey him, but put to sea. When they had left the land about two hours the storm became far stronger, and some of the sailors insisted they should go back, but my lord called them cowards, (he feared nothing himself at any time, and when he thought he would soon see me if he kept on, it was not possible he would be afraid and return,) and insisted the ship's course should not be changed. As the seamen found my lord would not be disobeyed, they steered on for Dover; but a sudden fierce gust of wind so tore the sails and the cordage that the ship was almost a wreck on the waters. Now they had not the power to return if they would, but they continued on as they best could. (Ah, me! would they had never left Calais, whither they had all arrived in perfect safety!) Though the ship rolled terribly, and they were much embarrassed with the cordage—as it was, they could do nothing—my lord's courage never left him, and he animated the seamen and spoke comfortably to the men-at-arms, saying they would soon be in England with their wives and families. And the sea continued to roll over the vessel in a fearful manner, and the helmsman was tied to the ship so that he could not be washed away. But it was only in the power of Heaven to help them, for by no human skill did it appear possible.—In the meantime, the rowers in the little boat pulled manfully against the waves. . . . . My dear lord was dead.

CHAPTER VII.

THE terrible shock caused by the news of my husband's death threw me for some months on a bed of sickness. At first the intelligence weighed on me so oppressively that I lay in a sort of stupor; not asleep, yet far from awake. I knew perfectly well my loss, yet it seemed too stupendous for me to realise. I did not pray— not that I would not willingly have sought consolation in prayer, but I could not frame my mind consecutively for a time on any one thing. I afterwards heard that I sometimes talked foolishly about things of no interest to me, and which did not relate to me or the deep sorrow I was in, and this would sometimes continue for days together.

At last I recovered my mind, and a total change of thought and behaviour took place within me. I was no longer dulled to the terrible misfortune which had occurred to me; on the contrary, I felt it in its full force. My eyes from being dry and hot were now so full of tears that all around me pitied me and tried to console me, though without success, for my sorrow was too great to listen to reason. I wept for my lord as a loving wife would weep who had lost so noble a treasure. I say not this to my own praise, for it was but natural, and it would have been a mortal sin not to have felt for such a husband as I felt for mine; but to the greater glory of God, who had in His bounty restored to me my full love for my lord, as my sorrow amply proved.

For some weeks I remained with my room darkened, that

I might think of him I had lost the more readily, and that I might pray the more perfectly for strength to support my misfortune. I tried humbly to resign myself to the blow that Heaven in its wisdom had struck me, nor question the justice of its will. By degrees my mind became calmer, and I allowed Bertha, who had attended me in my affliction, both bodily and mental, with more than the love of a sister, to open the curtains of my chamber and let in the light of day. It was a bright, beautiful day when she did so, and when the flood of light from the glorious sun poured into the room through the casement I felt more happy, for it almost seemed as if the eye of God himself looked in upon me in my sorrow. Presently I asked Bertha to give me my mirror, but she delayed and said she had mislaid it, so I told her to bring me one from another room. I then found out the truth. "Dear lady," said she, "do not look into the mirror, for you are sorely changed."

But I commanded her to bring me my own mirror, which she did. When I looked into it, I was much surprised how altered my face was. I, who naturally was ruddy, was now ghastly pale, and my eyes wanted brightness and were sunk deep into my head; and, beyond that, I looked many years older. But I was not in any way sorry.

"My fairness and youth are both gone," I said, "but I rejoice thereat; it is just my beauty should be buried in the grave of my husband."

I now began to question Bertha about her sister, for hitherto my grief had made me selfish, and I had thought only of my own sorrow. The poor woman's husband and two other men-at-arms had perished with my lord; the others had been saved. I found, as was natural, that the loss of her husband, so soon following that of her child, had been almost fatal to her with her ill-health; but that now she was better, and also her knee no longer pained her, (thanks to the skill of the priest,) and although it was still very weak, she hoped soon to be able to walk. I inquired what she intended to do when she had recovered her health. Bertha told me she wished her sister to live with her, and intended proposing such an arrangement to her husband; but that she dreaded his answer, as, although he was both a good and generous man, he liked to be without other society than hers in his house, and she feared his refusal.

I asked her whether her sister would like to live with me as my servant.

Bertha said immediately that she was sure her sister would readily do so, but, at the same time, I noticed the girl's eyes fill with tears, and I asked her what ailed her.

She told me that although she dearly loved her sister, (as I well knew,) she did not like any one being near me but herself, as she feared I should forget her.

"You silly girl," I said, "you have a husband to attend to, and that is your duty; and besides, I can never again treat you as a servant, but as my friend." And here, forgetting my position, I kissed the dear girl, who was much pleased at my condescension, and told me she would tell her sister of my goodness, which she did; and it was arranged that as soon as she was well enough, she should leave her cottage and dwell with me as my servant in the castle.

(She never afterwards left me, but entered the convent the same time as myself. She was the lay sister Elizabeth, who died about six years since.)

Six months more passed over quietly. Though the first burst of my grief had somewhat subsided, my regret for my husband was as profound as ever. Various doubts now came before me. I could not understand that with my blessed rosary given to me by my lord, and which had worked such miracles, how it was he, who had been so good, was drowned when he had nearly joined me, whom he loved so well. My punishment I could understand, but not his. Still I would not doubt the wisdom and justice of Heaven; but I wished so much to be enlightened on that point, that I determined to write to the holy priest of St Botolph, asking him to visit me at the castle, that I might converse with him on the subject.

In due time I received his answer. He told me he would willingly oblige me if it were in his power, but at that moment it would be utterly impossible for him to leave his parish. There was not only much poverty but great sickness as well, and it behoved him as a soldier of the cross not to leave the battle in the hour of difficulty and danger. Possibly in a short time things would change for the better, and then he would willingly accept the offer I had made him. At the same time, I should bear in mind that if anything obliged me to take a journey to London, he would be happy on all occasions to give me his advice, spiritual or temporal.

The receipt of this letter gave me great cause for consideration. I had received more than one summons from my husband's scrivener relative to his will, (for my dear lord had left me much wealth,) and in these letters he had said that my presence in London was indispensable; but I had hitherto felt so great a disinclination to move from the castle, that I had each time evaded the summons. Now I was, on the contrary, willing to go: for I much wished to confess me to the holy priest and obtain his advice for my future guidance. So I resolved I would visit London for that purpose, and transact my business at the same time. I therefore wrote to my scrivener to provide me a house for a few weeks in some quiet neighbourhood, where I could maintain a perfect privacy during my stay. He obeyed my request; and in a few days I started with Elizabeth and two serving-men for London.

When I arrived, I found my scrivener had obtained for me a small house in the country near the village of Charing, but a short distance from London, and from whence I could go to the city whenever my presence was required there, either to see my confessor or to transact whatever business relating to my husband's death I was required to do. This pleased me greatly, as I much wished to see no one of my acquaintance during my sojourn; and now I could carry out my wishes without difficulty.

The second day after my arrival in London I went to the Church of St Botolph, in Bishopgate, and fortunately saw the good priest, although he was leaving the church at the time I entered. He immediately recognised me, and seemed much pleased at the meeting. I told him I had come to London almost purposely to see him and obtain his advice and instruction. He said he would willingly render it to me after my confession, and he then promised he would be in the confessional the next day one hour before noon, and he would reserve himself specially for me. He then left me, and I, after attending a mass in one of the chapels, went to my home.

The next morning, after having duly prepared myself with prayer to the best of my ability, I went to the church in Bishopgate and presented myself at the confessional. Fully and humbly I there laid open my transgressions to the holy priest; nothing did I conceal that I could possibly remember. My sins of omission were great, and if those of commission were less in number, there was one which terrified me exceedingly—I doubted the justice of God in punishing my dear husband for my fault.

The priest listened patiently and attentively. When I had concluded, he did not speak so comfortably to me as he did when I formerly confessed to him. He told me it was a great sin on my part to doubt the justice of Heaven in allowing the death of my husband, and that he had not been punished for my fault : that his death was no more than all had to pass through; and that the short time he could have stopped on earth, had he lived, was but as a moment to the eternity of bliss which awaited him. The punishment—and a just one it was, like all the judgments of Heaven—was on me. He saw that Satan had still great power over me, and had deceived my mind in persuading me that it was my husband's punishment that I grieved for, when it was almost wholly my own disappointment that I felt.

He then inquired how I had passed the time since my lord's death, and what masses I had put up for the repose of his soul.

I also answered these questions candidly. I told him for many weeks after my lord's death I continued very sick both in body and mind, and kept my chamber the while. Afterwards by degrees I recovered, and then I offered up masses for his soul, but not many, for I did not much trust the priest of our parish; not that I did not believe him to be a good man, and would willingly have advised me on all things to the best in his power, but that I rather looked at him as a man skilful in curing diseases than as one learned as a priest. I told him also that I had occupied my time in occasional good works and frequent prayer. The priest then asked me what good works I had done, and what my means were to exercise charity.

I considered for a moment, and then was so ashamed of the truth that I hesitated to speak it. With the exception of Bertha, who required but little at my hands, her sister, the old woman who had been reputed a witch, and a few others whom I had assisted, I had done nothing. But as I intended to make a full confession I would not conceal anything, so I told the priest the whole truth, and shewed him how little I had done. I further told him that my dear husband had left me great wealth, but of what amount I did not know, for as yet I had taken but little account of it.

The priest then told me that my conduct had been but little acceptable to God. That with great means at my disposal I had done but little good; that I had not taken sufficient care in obtaining the aid of the Holy Church for the welfare of my dear husband's soul, and that I had been too much occupied in the indulgence of my own selfish sorrow. Also, that although grief for the loss of one so beloved was both natural and commendable, to succumb to it unreasonably, to the prejudice of the poor and the neglect of the Church, was not a virtue, but a fault.

I told him I was much grieved at the blame he had cast on me, and that I would faithfully follow whatever advice or instruction he should give me.

He advised me to enter a convent for some months, passing the time in frequent prayer and occasional fasting, giving alms of all I had to the poor, and causing masses to be offered up for the repose of my husband's soul.

He then inquired if I knew any one connected with any convent who would advise me in which to pass the time during my retirement.

I told him the holy Lady Edith Barogh, abbess of the Benedictine Convent at Wilton, was my own cousin, and although I had not seen her since I was a child, still I was certain she would willingly receive me if I wished it.

He advised me immediately to write to her, which I promised to do. I then told him I was also occupied in London with my scrivener about some of my lord's affairs—did he wish me to enter the convent immediately, or to wait till all was concluded? He told me to wait; that it was just, and not against God's will, that proper attention should be given to worldly affairs while we were in the world. My confession shortly afterwards concluded, and I then went to my home.

My first care the next day was to write a long letter to my cousin, the Abbess of Wilton. In it I told her of the sad and terrible misfortune which had overwhelmed me. I described how noble a gentleman was my husband, and how necessary it was for me to shew a proper respect for his memory; that I had remained for some months at the castle overwhelmed with my grief, doing little for the benefit of my dear husband's soul, and less for my own; how that I had been obliged by important business to visit London, and that during my sojourn there I had confessed to the good priest of St Botolph, and that he had advised me to pass some months in seclusion in the practice of prayer and good works, and the offering up of frequent masses for the repose of the soul of my dear lord. I further told her that if she would allow me to be a pensioner with her during the period, it would give me great pleasure, as I had not only a great respect for her but the holy house of which she was herself the Superior.

In less than a week I received her answer, so much haste did my good messenger make. My cousin told me she would willingly receive me and give me all the accommodation the convent afforded. She further said the confessors of the convent and the priests of Wilton were good and holy men, who would assist me in all things where their spiritual advice would be of service to me. Also, that there were many poor in Wilton and the neighbouring city of Salisbury, as well as the surrounding villages, and that I could have abundant opportunities to exercise my charities, not only in relieving the poor in their miseries, but in aiding by gifts the work of godly teaching and instruction to their children as well. She concluded by saying that she hoped the quiet and seclusion of their house, assisted by my own and the sisterhood's prayers, would restore me again to my former peace of mind, and that she looked forward with impatience to the day she should see me.

This letter I answered by another, thanking her for her kind compliance of my request, and telling her that as soon as the necessary affairs I was engaged in were concluded I would write to her, informing her of the possible day of my arrival. I then waited on the good priest, and told him of the arrangement I had made. He said I had done well, and that I should write to him and inform him of my health when I was at Wilton, and that if ever I visited London again, and he should be alive, he would always be happy to see me and afford me every advice in his power. I then left with him some good alms for his poor, and some money for the purposes of his church, for all of which he thanked me, and I then left him; nor did I see him again, for he died a few months afterwards.

I remained for some weeks in London; for the affairs of my lord were long before they were brought to a satisfactory conclusion. The sojourn did my mind great good; for the desponding sorrow I had hitherto felt, if it did not vanish, was greatly lessened. I now saw more clearly my position. While waiting for the answer of my cousin the abbess, I left the house but seldom; but now I had received it, and had resolved to remain with her in the practice of prayer and good works for six months, I thought it would not be contrary to my duty as a widowed wife, or my respect to my dear husband, if I went occasionally to London to view the streets and the shops, and the rich things they contained. On these occasions I was always accompanied by the wife of my scrivener—a staid and discreet person, but one who knew London well, and all the best merchants. Although I greatly admired what I saw, I bought but few things, as I had no wish to wear rich apparel during my widowhood; and I thought it would be time enough to think of such vanities after my sojourn in the convent was over. I bought a handsome dress and coif as a present for Bertha, and several other things for the different domestics at the castle, all of whom had behaved to me during my sorrow with great respect and consideration.

I went nowhere into society: I thought it would not be respectful to the memory of my dear lord. The wife of my scrivener, nevertheless, tempted me often, and told me that now I had been a widow for so many months and had maintained the while so severe a seclusion, I might now mix again with the world, especially as I was about to enter a convent for so long a time, where I should have but little to relieve my mind; but I resisted all her reasons and entreaties, and maintained my determination. She more than once asked me if I would attend the court, as the king might be offended if he heard that a lady of my position had been so long in London and had not waited on the queen; but I told her that my recent widowhood would always stand a good excuse for me, and I would not go. Furthermore, I had another reason, of which I did not speak to her, nor hardly would I whisper it to myself—I feared meeting those there whom it was my duty to avoid.

At last the scrivener had finished the whole of my affairs, and I made preparations for my departure. I did not then write to the abbess as I had resolved, for I had obtained the consent of my confessor, first to return to the castle and make arrangements how things should be conducted during my absence, as well as to say farewell to all my faithful dependents.

The day before we started I received a letter, brought by a man who had left it without waiting for any answer or making any remark. With some surprise, but no trepidation, I opened it, and was greatly annoyed to find it was from the Vidame. How he had contrived to know of my sojourn in London I know not; for I had made myself but little conspicuous, purposely that I should not be recognised. For some time I remained with the letter open in my hand, hardly knowing what to do with it; but my woman's curiosity (I say it with penitence and shame) overcame me, and I read the contents. There was nothing in the letter in any way to offend me. He commenced by saying how deep his sorrow was for the accident to my dear lord, and that he sympathised with me in my misfortune. He went on to state that he hoped I would no longer seclude myself from the world, and he prayed respectfully permission that he might call on me.

I have candidly admitted that I did wrong in reading the letter. With equal honesty, I assert it neither gave me pleasure nor pain—that it was, in fact, indifferent to me. When I had finished it, without anger I tore it in pieces, threw it on the ground, and thought no more about it.

The next morning we started homewards. As we left, I turned round to look at the great city in the distance. It was obscured in the mist of the morning, and was not clearly to be seen. I then turned without a pang or regret that I should leave it, and continued my journey homewards, and in three days we arrived safely at the castle.

CHAPTER VIII.

IT would be difficult for me to describe the pleasure which came over me when I again entered my home. I felt not only a sensation of peace, but even of happiness; and had not a sacred duty obliged me, I would willingly have avoided my sojourn in the abbey—a most wicked thought, for which I have done good penance since. My servants came around me, and testified so much joy at my return, that I easily forgave the almost rudeness they shewed in my presence. I inquired of one after the other of the news of their families, and was, in truth, greatly interested and pleased with their answers; for they all shewed, by the certainty of the interest I felt in them, that they believed I loved them; while, at the same time, I was their lady and mistress. When they had concluded their different stories, I ordered one of the boxes which had been taken from the pack-horses to be brought into the room and opened, and from it I took divers presents I had brought for them. For the women there were coifs and cloaks and gowns, and knives for the men; for they held the London knives in great estimation there, as we hold those of Salisbury here. I then gave them to the different servants, each according to his standing, at which they were all pleased; indeed, they shewed so much joy in their faces, that I did not like to tell them I was so soon to leave them again. Neither Bertha nor her husband were there. They had not heard of our arrival—for it was evening before we got to the castle—but I heard they were both in good health, for which I was thankful. As last the servants left me, and when they were all gone I said my prayers somewhat hurriedly, for I was sorely tired, and went to bed.

The next morning my first visit was from the parish priest. It gave me great pleasure to see him, for he was good to the poor, and he could tell me all that had passed among them during my absence. He had, I am happy to say, no bad accounts to give me. It is true, some of the peasants had been unfortunate with their gardens and fowls, and other little things, but in which he had assisted them, (before I left the castle I gave him instructions to bestow alms and assistance to the poorest among them, and when he wanted help he was to apply to my steward, who would always aid him,) so there was no great mischief done. He likewise told me the old woman, whom we had taken for a witch, was very infirm, but that she wanted for nothing, as he had obeyed my instructions in sending her food, raiment, and fuel. He also said she now carried herself very discreetly, in no way interfering with the sick poor, but that she was a constant attendant at mass, and conducted herself very devoutly. He had praised God often, he said, that we had prevented her, by means of my blessed rosary, from being drowned, as he was now certain she was no witch, but an ignorant old woman, who formerly had done harm without intending it.

After he had left me, Bertha and her husband came to the castle. Like the rest, the man seemed pleased to see me, but Bertha shewed by her face the delight she had in my presence, though she had the good sense not to kiss me before her husband. I talked with him for some time, and he told me about his cows and sheep, and other things connected with his farm, all of which I made pretence to take great interest in, to please him, though in reality I cared but little about them. When he had finished I told him I was pleased to hear he was so prosperous, and I gave him a pair of shears for his sheep, which I had bought in London of a merchant for him, who was highly skilled in tools of the kind. He seemed much pleased not only at the shears but at my remembrance of him, and praised them very highly. I let him go on a little longer, and then I told him I hoped he would leave Bertha with me for the day, as I had much to talk to her about. He willingly did as I desired, and shortly after left us.

I then took Bertha into my inner chamber, and we talked a long time together. I then told her I intended going into the convent at Wilton for at least six months, to pass the time in seclusion. She was much grieved to hear it, for she said she had hoped I would have stopped with them. I told her it was only for a few months, and then she would see me again; but she shook her head, and said that if once I entered the walls of that holy house they would make me so happy I should never leave it again. I endeavoured to persuade her she was wrong, and that I did not intend to reside there, but she would not credit me, but began to cry; whereupon, to console her, I thought I would present her with the handsome gown and coif I had bought for her in London.

Without telling her my intention, I went to the chest and drew them out. When she saw them she said, "My dear lady, how happy I am to see you are no longer going to wear black; you will look so well in those handsome things. Now I see them, I will believe you do not intend stopping in the convent."

When I told her they were not for me, but that I had bought them for her to wear, she seemed greatly surprised, and could hardly believe me; but when I repeated it the tears immediately dried in her eyes, and they beamed with pleasure. I was much grieved to see how pleased she was with such vanities; and I almost regretted I had bought them, for, as I said before, Bertha was very pretty and too fond of dress; but I could not take them back, so I remonstrated with her on the subject.

I told her how wrong it was to set her heart on vanities of the kind, and that it grieved me to see it, for there was great danger in it; that Satan frequently made use of fine dress to ensnare the soul, and that it was dangerous to all, but especially to those in her position in life; and that I hoped she would wear the gown and coif with all humility, and not think much of herself on that account, which I feared she would do.

Bertha listened very demurely to my remonstrance, and said she had no doubt I was quite right, and that I knew best, she was sure, and much more of the same sort; but I could mark that her eye looked with pleasure on the gown and coif the while, and that my good advice had but little effect.

While I was sorrowful in mind that my good advice had not benefited Bertha, for I loved the girl notwithstanding her vanity, I was told that the old woman who had been accused of witchcraft, and so nearly punished for it, waited in the hall to see me. I arose from my seat, from which I had been silently looking out of my casement, and went into the hall. Bertha accompanied me, to my great pleasure, leaving the gown and coif on the table. As soon as the old woman saw me enter, she advanced to meet me. She appeared much changed, so much so that I should hardly have known her. She was much more infirm, for now she could walk but with great difficulty, and she bent very much. Formerly, though very old, she was active, and could do something to aid others as well as herself; but now she appeared to have no strength left, not even sufficient to support and tend upon herself. At the same time, I liked much better the expression of her countenance; though deadly pale, there was a pious, resigned intelligence in it, quite different from the haggard, angry look she wore the first day I saw her. She was also neatly dressed, which pleased me much, for although it had been furnished by my steward, it was such as an old woman ought to wear, quiet in colour, but warm and comfortable.

Finding the poor creature, though supported by her staff, had great difficulty in walking, I went up to her and took her by the hand, intending to lead her to a seat, but she would not let me. She let her staff fall on the ground, and tried to kneel, but I prevented her. She then stooped, and taking my dress in her hands kissed it reverently, which I attempted to prevent, but in vain. As soon as she could find words she said, "Dear lady, how can I thank you for all your goodness to me? You have been an angel to me, and have saved me by your kindness from three deaths—from drowning, from starving, and from sickness, (I had heard from the priest who had attended her that she had been very ill, and the marks of her malady were still visible in her pallid face.) You have given me life and time to pray, and I do so; but it mostly is for Heaven to shower its blessings on you for your goodness."

When I heard this, I rebuked the old woman for her impiety. Her thoughts, I told her, ought to be on Heaven on her own account, and not on mine. I, though a lady, was in the eye of God a poor sinful creature like herself, and I was fully content with what I had done in seeing her so comfortable.

"But still, dear lady," she said, "it was you that saved me from that terrible death; had it not been for your goodness I should have been killed for a witch, when God knows I was totally innocent."

I told her she was in error, and that I had not saved her

life, but had only been a humble instrument in the hands of Heaven; that her life had been saved by the blessed rosary which I bore, and not by me; that it was by its influence she was rescued, and by no power of mine.

I then detached the rosary from my side and placed it in her hands. She first crossed herself, and then kissed it reverently several times, and then she returned it to me. That done, Bertha picked up her staff for her, and assisted her to a seat by the window, where also I ordered a table to be placed by it, with some food upon it; and while she was eating I conversed with her, and obtained from her much information respecting her manner of living and former life.

Although her history is unconnected with my confession, I may mention that she had passed through much sorrow. She had lived happily enough till her husband had been taken by his lord (she then lived in a distant part of the country) to the king's wars. From that time her misfortunes began. Her husband was killed in the first battle he was in. She had then four children, three sons and one girl. Her eldest boy, who was seventeen years of age, was then taken by the lord to supply the place of the father; the girl, however, had married a respectable man who lived on my dear lord's father's estate. Before the end of the year, the eldest son was killed; and the other, a boy of fifteen, was too young to be a soldier, and he remained with the mother for two years longer. He was then taken, and the poor woman never saw him afterwards; whether he was killed or made prisoner she knew not. She then fell into great distress, and with difficulty found her way across the country to her daughter, who was then a widow. She afterwards maintained herself by nursing and tending the sick till her daughter's death, after which she had struggled on as she best could.

Others called upon me also on that day; but as they do not concern my narrative, I omit mentioning them specially.

In the early part of the next morning, I was occupied with my steward, making arrangements for the management of my estates during my seclusion in the convent. As all was in good order, this gave me but little difficulty, the more so as my steward was a most honourable man, and one in whose judgment I could place full reliance. In the afternoon, I wrote a letter to my cousin, the Lady Abbess of Wilton, telling her I was now ready to enter her house if she could admit me, and that as soon as I received her answer I would leave the castle. Also that, if she answered me immediately, I should be with her, God willing, about the middle of the next week. I then despatched a messenger with the letter.

While I awaited the answer of the Abbess, I occupied my time partly with the affairs of my estate, but more so with making arrangements for the well-being of the poor and needy during my absence. In this the good priest aided me greatly. His counsel was of much use in shewing me how I could dispense my charity, while the steward, with his more worldly and prudent advice, guided me on the side of caution. At last the letter arrived, and I found, as I had anticipated, that my cousin longed to see me; and I determined (it was mid-day when I received the letter) to leave home the next morning. I immediately gave to my servants the necessary orders for our journey the next day, and that the pack-horses with the luggage should set forward several hours before us, so that they might be at the halting-place for the night before we had reached it. We were to sleep the first day at a village a half day's journey from Wilton, so that I might arrive at the convent about mid-day.

As soon as my orders were given, and my servants occupied in making preparations for the morrow, I strolled from the castle with the intention of visiting some of the spots where the principal occurrences had taken place before my lord's death, and which I, with a sort of reverential fear, had abstained from visiting since. I first directed my steps to the scene of the old woman's ordeal. I know not why I should have taken the path I did, for it was far longer than the one I ordinarily should have chosen, though it avoided the pathway across which the great tree had fallen in the night of the storm. After waiting on the spot for some time, and wondering at the great virtues of my rosary, I visited the cottage of the old woman herself. I found her very feeble, but cheerful and contented. She told me she knew how ill she was, but she did not dread the termination. Up to the present moment she had daily attended mass, in gratitude for my kindness to her, and Heaven's mercy in saving her from an infamous death. As long as she could continue this, she wished to live; but as soon as weakness had deprived her of the power, she trusted that Heaven in its mercy would take her speedily afterwards. I looked round her cottage to see if there was anything necessary for her I could send her, but there appeared no lack of requisites, so I wished her good day and better health. I never saw her again; she died suddenly about a month afterwards.

I then went to the cottage of Bertha's sister. Some people were living in it whom I did not know. They knew me, however, and received me with great respect, and requested me to enter, which I did. But all was changed. There was nothing to remind me of the sad scenes which had taken place in it; and although Bertha's sister was known to them, they knew only of the infant's death from hearsay, having lived till lately in a very distant part of my lord's estate. I left the cottage much depressed in spirit; for the change appeared to me so great, that all that there had taken place should be so soon forgotten.

I then bent my steps to the churchyard, and visited the grave of the poor baby. I was much surprised and grieved at the state it was in. No attention had been paid to it; not a flower had been planted on it, and the rains which had fallen had washed the spot nearly level with the surrounding ground. I had felt too deeply for the poor baby not to remember well the grave in which it was laid; but had I not attended the funeral, I should not have found it, so completely had the traces of the spot been obliterated. At first I felt angry with the mother for the neglect she had shewn to the body of her child; but then I remembered that she had kindly tended it in its illness, and wept bitterly its death. I thought that perhaps the news of her husband's death had made her grieve less for her child, so I forbore to judge harshly of her. At the same time, I had not the same good feeling for her I had for Bertha, who, had she been of gentle blood, would have been much beloved by all, while her sister had more of the churl about her; nevertheless, she was a good and faithful servant.

I now bent my steps homeward. This time I took the shortest path, which led past the fallen tree, and the spot on which I stood the eventful evening of the storm. When I arrived, I found the huge tree still barred the passage—it having fallen, as I before said, across the narrow road. I stopped when I arrived at it, and mused on the manner I had escaped destruction in its fall, and I again thanked Heaven that I had in my possession the blessed rosary, by whose virtue I had been saved. I stayed some time by the tree; for the evening was calm and beautiful, and well adapted for thought. Presently the idea occurred, that the fall of the tree now prostrate before me had been a forewarning from Heaven of the death of my dear lord; for as he was the most noble among men, so was the tree which had fallen the most noble in the surrounding wood. The more I reflected on the comparison the more clear it appeared to me, till at last I began to entertain the same respect for it I should have done for a sculptured monument in some noble church to his memory. The feeling increased, till at last I prayed before it as I would have done at an altar, my beads which he had sent me being in my hand the while. When I had concluded I rose from my knees and walked reverently round the tree, wondering in my mind how I could do something with it that should be typical of my noble lord; and this idea continued to occupy my mind till I had arrived at the castle.

When I was near the gates, I found many of my servants assembled, with sorrow marked on their countenances. Though I noticed it, no sensation of fear came over me, for I had now personally little to care for; but thinking that some misfortune might have befallen one of their number, I called the porter aside to me to ask him what their sorrow might mean. He told me it arose from their knowledge of my departure on the morrow, for which they were all much grieved; so I advanced towards them and told them that I should be but a few months absent, and when I should return to them again, I hoped never more to leave them. This in some way consoled them, but still they looked very sadly.

When I arrived in my private chamber I sent Elizabeth for my steward, requesting him to wait on me immediately. He did so, and as soon as we were alone I told him I wished to speak to him about the fallen tree. He told me it was his intention soon to remove it, and he would have done so before had not all the men in the neighbourhood been lately occupied in getting in the harvest. I informed him I would in nowise have it removed, and that I wanted him to tell me whether it would be possible to alter the course of the present road, so as to allow the fallen tree to lie in the position it was now in.

"Nothing would be more easy," was his reply; "but the timber in the tree is of value, and it is a pity to let it be wasted."

I was so angry at his answer that for some time I could

not speak. The steward the while looked at me with astonishment, wondering what offence he could have given me. When I had recovered myself I told him that it was my wish, as well as my strict order, that not a branch should be taken from that tree, and that all the peasants around should be informed of my determination; that it should remain there with as much respect as if it had been a church monument; that a road should immediately be commenced that should go around it, and from time to time that he, the steward, should visit the tree and see that no harm was done to it.

The steward seemed surprised at my order, but promised I should be obeyed. I did not relieve him from his surprise by any explanation on my part, but I allowed him to retire.

(Though I never afterwards saw the tree, I ascertained, on good authority, that my orders were faithfully carried out, and that the tree remains there to this day.)

CHAPTER IX.

I ROSE early the next morning, and after offering up my accustomed prayers, I opened my casement and gazed out on the country. The sun was shining in full splendour, and the whole scene it lighted was bright, peaceful, and beautiful. As I viewed it, my heart throbbed with pleasure, for I felt it shewed the contentment of Heaven at the step I was about to take; that it blest the journey with its approbation, and that its end would tend to the greater honour of God and my own spiritual welfare. Never was prophecy more perfectly fulfilled than in my own personal case; for it was the commencement of an era in my existence which greatly tended to my own happiness and peace of mind—although at the commencement I had occasion to dread a terrible result, and that the brilliant augury of the morning threatened to terminate in a terrible night.

I remained in my private chamber till I had breakfasted, and then I attended mass, which was celebrated by the parish priest at an altar fitted up in a small chapel in the castle, and at which no one attended but Bertha and myself; for she had left her home at an early hour with the intention of accompanying me for some miles on the road.

When the mass was over, I gave orders that the horses should be prepared, which occupied some time, rather because the grooms were talking with their friends, whom they were about to leave, than for necessity; for most things had been prepared the evening before, and the sumpter-horses had started that morning before daylight.

At last they told me the horses waited at the gate of the castle, and that all was in readiness. I then left my private chamber and descended to the hall, where I found all my servants congregated to wish me adieu. I felt both pleased and sad at the affection they shewed me. They wished me all happiness and a prosperous and pleasant journey, as well as a speedy return. Nor were they vain words they uttered, for the expression of their faces shewed them to be in earnest. I told them it was my intention to return to them as soon as my sojourn in the convent should be terminated, and that during my absence I would daily pray for them.

This appeared to please them greatly, and many asked me individually to pray for them, (for in so holy a house they justly believed that prayers would be heard; and, moreover, they knew the great sanctity of Salisbury, with its famous cathedral and shrines, which was near, and they rightly supposed I would often visit it.) I readily promised I would do as they desired. They all asked me also to pray for them. As I wished to please them, but could not remember all they asked me, I requested Bertha to get me a pen that the priest might make a note for me of their several demands; but Bertha, who was very sad, would not stir from my side, but asked another to get it instead. When it was brought, the priest kindly made the note for me, and I put it in my pocket, promising them all I would do as they wished: and I faithfully kept my word.

We now went to the castle gate, where the horses were waiting for us. Here I found a great number of the tenants and peasants had assembled to bid me adieu. There were so many that I had great difficulty in relieving myself from them, for though I could have done so, had I acted harshly or abruptly, yet I was loath to do so when they shewed me so much good-will. In time, however, I had bid each adieu, and we proceeded to mount our horses.

Several who did not belong to our party accompanied me for some miles; among others, the priest, and Bertha and her husband, all of whom were on horseback. The priest rode at my right hand and Bertha at my left, her husband and Elizabeth following us. The others rode as it pleased them best. There was little conversation among us, for though all, with the exception of Bertha, tried to smile and appear happy, they did not succeed, nor was I displeased at it, for it told me they loved me, and were sorry for my departure, even more clearly than words could have done. Still, onward we went, and the bright sun shone on us, and lighted us up gaily in spite of our sadness.

When we had left the castle about two hours, I commanded the party to halt. I then told the priest, Bertha, and the rest of the party who were not to go on with us, I was much pleased at the affection they had shewn me, but that now I would release them from further attendance on me. They offered some objections, but I was imperative, and they prepared to obey me. One by one I bade them adieu, till Bertha alone remained. When I bade her farewell, the poor girl could not restrain herself, but, forgetting the difference in our grades, she embraced me as well as she could, being on horseback, and I kissed her heartily and affectionately in return. I then waited quietly till they had turned their horses' heads homewards and had proceeded some distance on their way, when I continued my own journey onwards.

We continued on our way silently and sadly. There was no one of my escort with whom I could converse. The only woman I had with me was Elizabeth, but, as I before stated, she was a very different woman from Bertha; for although honest, willing, and obedient, there was no sympathy between us. We halted at noon for our dinner and to refresh the horses, who were somewhat jaded with the heat of the sun, for it was very hot. We rested in the hostelry for more than two hours, during which time I remained alone in a chamber, for I felt lonely and sad at leaving my home and those I loved so well; and to talk with strangers at such a moment seemed intolerable. In the meantime, my servants refreshed the horses and made themselves happy with the host, which rather annoyed me at the time, I felt so miserable; but I afterwards thought it was quite natural for them to do so, as they would be but a few days from home, while I should have to remain some months. Little did I imagine that I should never return, and what occurrences would arise to induce me to take the veil and reside continually in the convent.

About three hours after mid-day, we again started on our journey. The men would willingly have waited longer, but we had a long distance before us, and the country was rather wild. There were now few houses to be seen, and none for the entertainment of travellers; indeed, at the village at which we were to pass the night, there was none, and a cottage had to be hired by my servants for our accommodation. It was nearly sunset when we arrived, and we were all much tired. I found my servants, whom I had sent forward, as well as the owners of the cottage, had done their best for my comfort; and I was well pleased with them for their good intentions, though it was hardly necessary, as I am by no means fastidious or delicate.

After I had a little rested and taken some refreshment, I was told that the priest of the village waited on me, and wished to see me. Although fatigued, and wishing to be at peace, I had not the heart to refuse him, so I ordered him to be admitted, and a light to be brought in.

He was an old man, very poor, and very humble. He

moreover appeared very ignorant, though much interested in his parishioners, all of whom, he said, were in great poverty. Their harvest had been very bad; and he said that the harvest moon, which was then at its full, had never shone on a poorer crop. I inquired of him how far it was to Wilton, and whether the road would be better than it had been to-day. He told me the distance was little more than half a day's journey, but that there was no road, the whole way being across a wide and uncultivated plain.

He then talked about the country in his neighbourhood, which, he said, was partly cultivated, and partly the wide plain he had spoken of. There was, he also said, at but a short distance from the village, a great circle of huge stones placed in a fantastical manner upon each other, of which nothing of its origin was known. Some said it was formerly a temple to false gods, built by savages and heathens, but that others thought it was the work of the Evil One himself. To this opinion he said he inclined, for the stones were so large, they could not have been placed on each other by mortal hands.

I asked him if the spot were near at hand. He told me it was, but he would not advise me to visit it after dark, for it had a bad reputation for evil spirits, and that he had heard often of their appearance, but he had never seen any himself, (perhaps they would not appear to him on account of his holy calling,) nor had he ever met with any person who had had direct communication with them, although he knew many who knew others that had seen them. If, however, I should like to visit the spot the next morning, he would willingly accompany me.

I thanked him for his offer, without accepting it, determining that I would wait till the morrow before I made up my mind; not that I had any fear of evil spirits, but that my heart was sad, and I had but little curiosity about the matter.

I now inquired more especially into the state of the poor of his parish, and he gave me many sad instances of misery, sickness, and bitter poverty. I then questioned him as delicately as I could on his own resources, and soon found they were little better than his poor neighbours, and that his chapel was much dilapidated, and that his priest's vestments were sorely out of repair, and of many other things equally sad. When he left me, and it was then dark night, I placed in his hands wherewithal to relieve some of the pressing necessities of his flock, and also an offering for his church, and the proper celebration of its mysteries, as well as, with as little offence as I could, a present for himself, for all of which he expressed himself most grateful, and he left me, I believe, well pleased with his visit.

As it was now getting late, I began to prepare for my bed. The evening was warm and sultry, and I had hardly commenced undressing, when I thought I would open the little casement to let in the cooler air. As I did so, I remarked the great beauty of the night, for there was not a cloud in the heavens, and the full moon was shining brightly on the earth. I remained for some time with my elbow on the sill, gazing at the calm beauty of the scene. Notwithstanding that all was so lovely and quiet around me, my soul was not at ease. Although tired, and about to prepare for my bed, I had no inclination to sleep. I could not fix my thoughts on any one subject. One moment they were on the lovely scene before me, the next they were at the castle, and then they would turn to my visit to London, and my cottage at Charing.

Annoyed at this vacillation, I resolved to seek my bed, and for this purpose called to Elizabeth, who had for herself a small chamber behind mine. I waited for some time, but she did not answer me, so I took the lamp and went into her room to ascertain the cause of her silence. There I on a huge stone which had been cast upon the ground and looked calmly around me.

Soon the strangeness of the scene faded on my mind, and my thoughts returned to the current they had been in before. I saw the huge stones by which I was now surrounded. I felt now more displeased than before with the thought of my seclusion, and my mind became more rebellious. I turned over in my thoughts in what way I could shorten the time, and several excuses presented themselves to me; but, upon thinking on them, each one contained a falsehood and I rejected it, for although I was sorely tempted to act in a rebellious manner, I would not condescend to gain my ends by telling an untruth. At last, I resolved to remonstrate with my cousin when I should get tired of my sojourn with her, and beg her to use her influence with the Bishop of Salisbury, who was her spiritual superior, to allow me to leave the convent, which I could then do without letting the priest of St Botolph know of my return to my home.

I now turned my thoughts on my visit to London, and the various sights I had there seen. Strange at such a time I should have remembered the shops of the merchants, and the various rich jewels and dresses I had there seen, and in what manner they would become me did I wear them; and yet they occupied my mind for some time. Their memory brought me back to the time of my former sojourn in London, and the gay sights and feasts, and the music and the dancing that had been there. All appeared as bright, beautiful, and gay before me as at the time they occurred; but now I can remember with wonder, that not one thought of my dear Lord crossed my mind at the time, nor did the terrible miracle which had visited me in so marvellous a manner recur to my thoughts.

By degrees, and but for a moment at a time, the Vidame began to appear before me. Each time he dwelt longer and more distinctly on the memory. At last, I rather called for his presence than remained till it came. It appears to me, even at present, wonderful how clearly defined his features seemed to me. His handsome face, his smile, his quiet, respectful look of entreaty, his splendid form and dress—all were there as distinctly as if he had been present in person. I felt pleasure as I brought him to my memory, till, in the end, I thought I had done him an injustice. True, he had once been too bold; but he had never repeated the conduct. On the contrary, he had shewn the greatest sorrow for the fault he had committed; and I had forgiven him. Why should I entertain rancour towards him? He had written me a courteous letter, and I had not noticed it. Was that right on my part? He merely prayed that we might be again acquainted; and now I could do so without offence in the eyes of God or man. Why should I refuse? No; when I left the convent, should he again request it, I would allow his acquaintance.

This resolution had hardly crossed my mind when a sensation infinitely more hideous than when I first experienced the pressure of the hand at the king's feast now seized me. Loathsome as had been the contact of the former hand, this far exceeded it. So fearful, so nauseous was its effect, that, had not terror supported me, I should have fallen to the ground. I drew my hand away, but the horrible fingers clung to it, and their gentle pressure made them feel the more revolting. I moved from the spot I was standing on to another part of the circle, but the hand still retained its cold, clammy hold. I attempted to scream, but my voice failed me. Suddenly I bethought me of my rosary, and sought it with my left hand, but, to my intense horror, I had it not. What to do I knew not, and each moment I became more bewildered, for the horrible fingers still pressed mine with more entreating pressure. I then remembered the words of the old priest when he had mentioned the circle of stones to me, that they had been erected for the celebration of the worship of false gods by evil spirits. No sooner had the remembrance come to my mind, than I became distinctly aware of the presence of the fiends, that they surrounded me on every side. As I looked around me, in the deep shadows of the huge stones, I could perceive their hideous countenances. They glared at me from every side, but yet appeared as if they wished not to be seen; for, the instant my eye fell on the face of one of them, it vanished, while that of another yet more hideous appeared near it; or, if I turned away, they started forth in the shadow of some other stone. The scene was made even yet more horrible by the contrast of the pure moonlight which spread itself above me and around the circle, and its beams pierced through the interstices between the stones.

Presently my terror became so great that I sank upon the ground, the hand still pressing mine. I felt as if I should die; but the idea was so horrible that I should expire in so unholy a spot, that it seemed to give me a moment's energy. With my left hand I made the sign of the cross, and a moment's strength came to me. I then thought that if I rose from the dark shadow in which I lay, and placed myself in the light of the moonbeams, Heaven would afford me help. With a desperate effort, I half arose, and dragged myself into the moonlight. Already I felt stronger, and the countenances of the fiends became fewer. I crossed myself again and again, but always with my left hand, though now the sensation of the horrible pressure became less distinct. I now attempted to offer up a prayer to Heaven for aid; and I found it was heard, for my strength increased the moment it was uttered. I rose on my knees, and my courage returned to me, and I felt stronger. At last I stood erect, though I trembled violently. The pressure of the hand had now left me; but still the horrible, nauseous sensation caused by its touch continued. With my left hand I still crossed myself, (I did not dare to do so with the right, for it felt contaminated,) and my strength increased as I did so; but I had not the courage to run, for I feared passing through the black shadows, and again seeing the faces of the fiends. At last, half-closing my eyes, and praying to Heaven the while, I made the attempt. I was wonderfully supported in it, and at last I escaped from the enchanted circle.

Even when in the open country, my terror did not leave me. As I turned my back on the circle, I felt I dare not look round at it; but I ran towards the village as rapidly as I could, my breath almost failing me in my flight. As I got farther away from the circle, I found its attraction diminish, and my strength became somewhat greater. My mind also was more composed, and I stopped for a moment to offer up to Heaven a prayer for my escape; but I could not pray, probably, as I then thought, from the violent beating of my heart.

I now again continued my course, and in a short time I gained the entrance of the village; but my fear once more overtook me, for it was sheltered in trees, and very dark, and the remembrance of the deep shadows thrown by the huge stones again came before me. I now ran hurriedly on, my terror increasing as I advanced, till I had reached my own house, when it became insupportable. I attempted hurriedly to open the door, but could not succeed, whether from its being fastened, or by my unskilfulness, I know not. I got more alarmed as I found I could not enter, and I knocked loudly, but without success, for nobody heard me. Still, I knocked on with all my might, for I had a dreadful sensation that some one was behind me, but with no better effect. I exerted myself more and more to make myself heard, both by calling to Elizabeth and beating the door with my hands, but all without avail. At last my strength was unable to continue the exertion, and I fell senseless and exhausted on the ground.

CHAPTER X.

WAS aroused from my stupor by the voice of a man speaking kindly to me. I lifted my head, and found the day was fast breaking. I raised my eyes to the person who bent over me, and saw he was some poor husbandman, who had risen thus early to go to his daily labour. I told him I had in vain attempted to make myself heard the evening before, and that I had been obliged to remain where he found me through the night. He called my attention to the blood which covered my hands, as well as that on my face. I found that I had bruised myself in falling, and that my hands were much injured by the violence I had used in striking the door.

He now tried to awaken Elizabeth, and in a short time succeeded. When she opened the door and saw me, she sprang back from it with a scream, so altered and sad was the appearance I made. I entered the house, and she assisted me to undress, asking me questions the while, to all of which I gave no answer for I felt deadly sick and ill. When in bed I could not sleep, so great was the pain in my hands and face; nevertheless I remained quiet for some hours, and in time I felt somewhat restored.

When I arose in my bed, to my great joy I found my rosary, which I feared I had lost during my terror the previous evening, was safe at the head of my bed. I had placed it there in the evening, before determining on leaving the house. This gave me great consolation, as I felt a protecting hand was now over me.

In spite of Elizabeth's remonstrances I now arose, and washing the blood from my hands and face, I dressed myself as I best could, still feeling very sick. Before leaving my room, I looked for the kerchief I had placed on my head the evening before; but it was nowhere to be found. At first this caused me no regret, but as I thought more of it, I feared I might have left it within the circle of huge stones; and on reflection I had a vague idea that it had fallen from my head when first I became aware of the faces of the fiends glaring at me.

By degrees, however, the matter appeared to me in a different light, and that I should not allow any part of my garments to remain in so unholy a place, not knowing to what consequences it might lead. I then told Elizabeth to go immediately to the spot and seek for the kerchief; but she had overheard my conversation with the priest the evening before, and was afraid to go alone. Presently, I heard that the peasant who had found me at the door in the morning was outside, and I sent for him and asked him if he would accompany Elizabeth to the circle of great stones to find my handkerchief, which I had left there? He said he would go with her willingly; but that I must have great courage to remain in such a spot in the night, as he would not have done so for any reward. I made him no answer; but I thought how dreadful had been my danger when he, a man, was afraid to brave it. Elizabeth then consented to go with the peasant, and I remained at home awaiting their return.

The people of the cottage then brought me some breakfast; but my mouth was dry and parched, and I felt great nausea, as if the effect of the loathsome pressure of the dead hand had still its effect on me. They noticed also the bruises on my face and hands, and asked me what accident had happened to me; but I could not answer them, but began weeping. Seeing this, they asked me no more questions, but continued silent, removing the breakfast which I would not eat.

In a short time Elizabeth and the peasant returned to the cottage, but they had not found the kerchief. I now began to be frightened; so I sent for the parish priest, and asked him to wait on me, which he did immediately. When we were by ourselves, I told him I had been rash enough to walk out alone the evening before, and that I had strolled to the great circle of stones he had spoken of, and that I had there lost my kerchief, which I much wished to find—for I did not like to tell him how frightened I had been.

He said I must be a lady of great courage to venture to such a place alone; for even he, a minister of religion, would not have done so unless his duty had obliged him.

I made no answer to his remark, but told him he would do me a great favour if he would take what steps he could to recover my kerchief, and if he succeeded, to send it to me at Wilton Abbey. I gave him then further alms for his poor, and as a reward to any one who should find my kerchief, a gold ring of some value. He took the money and the ring, and readily promised to do all in his power to oblige me. I then ordered my men to prepare our horses to continue our journey to Wilton, but the priest and all around me advised me to remain in the cottage another day, as I was so ill. They were afraid, they said, the fatigue of the journey would make me worse; but I was resolved, and said I would go, ill as I was—nothing could persuade me to remain another night near that horrible place. I consented, however, to put off my departure till mid-day, to allow time for the kerchief to be found; but the delay was useless, for they could obtain no tidings of it.

It would be difficult to describe my great sorrow at the loss of my kerchief in such a place. A feeling came over me for which I could not account, it was so foolish—that the fiends had possession of it, and that I was in some way bound to them so long as they held it, and the doubt which existed was scarcely less painful than the reality. I begged the priest, who had already taken great pains to find it, to lose no opportunity, but to use what exertions he could, for the loss of it oppressed me greatly. He then inquired more particularly what sort of kerchief it was, and when I told him he hesitated for a moment, and then said that it did not appear to be of so much value as the gold ring. To this I made no answer, for it was true the kerchief was of little value, and I did not like to explain to him what was truly the reason of my desire to obtain it again.

When the horses were ready, I rose from my seat; but I was so weak I could hardly stand, and I was obliged to rest myself again. The priest once more advised me to remain in the cottage another night; but the very idea of being another day in that village gave me the strength to move, and, thanking him for his advice, I leant upon Elizabeth's arm, and walked to the door. With difficulty I was lifted on my horse, and I then thanked the priest for his good offices, and again impressed upon him my urgent wish to obtain the kerchief. He promised to take every opportunity to find it, and I then left him, and we went forward towards Wilton.

Although the afternoon was fine, and all around me appeared beautiful, it gave me no pleasure. I felt as if I had committed a great sin (which, doubtless, I had done); but I felt also as if my fault was too great to obtain pardon. Had I really sought the society of the terrible fiends I had seen the evening before, my sorrow and despair could not have been greater. I felt myself to be loathsome to all good Christians, and that repentance would not avail me. My eyes were dry; and although I would willingly have wept,

I could find no tears. I trembled as if with cold, and yet I felt a burning heat and thirst which was most painful. I would willingly have talked, and yet I had no inclination to speak. Besides, those of my escort would have been but of little use to me to console me, for they were all ignorant, though kind people. Oh, how I missed my dear Bertha! for though unlearned, I could open my heart to her, and she could have felt for me and have consoled me.

Onward we went, and the way appeared so long as to have no end, and each hour seemed longer than the last. As my fatigue increased, my irritation seemed to keep pace with it, and my thirst and heat increased in proportion, although the shuddering, as from cold, continued. From time to time I inquired of those few persons we met how far we were from the convent; yet although the distance they said was not long, the road seemed to me no shorter than before, so little progress did we appear to make, although my men assured me our pace was as fast as the horses could go.

At last, from the top of a high hill, we saw the convent and the town of Wilton. A change then came over me, and I felt so strong a desire to weep, I could not restrain myself, but gave full sway to my tears. From time to time, as we advanced, I dried for a moment my tears, and looked at the convent. It appeared so calm and holy in the light of the setting sun, that I urged on my horse to arrive the sooner. My men advised me not to go so quickly, as they feared I would fall—and, indeed, I rocked to and fro in my saddle from very weakness; but I paid them no attention, but went on as fast as before.

We came nearer to the town through which we had to pass before we could arrive at the convent. Then one of my men came forward, and asked me if he should ride on and let them know of my approach, thinking, in courtesy, some

A Legend of Wilton Abbey. 123

one would be sent by the lady abbess to meet me on the road. I made him no answer, but impatiently waved my hand to him to leave me, for which I was afterwards vexed, as he intended it civilly. I then heard my servants whispering together as we rode along. I knew they were talking about me, and I was angry with them for their presumption; but I said nothing, but looked anxiously at the town before me, wishing to arrive there.

Presently we entered it, and in a short time arrived by the market cross. I then felt I should like to dismount from my horse, and on my knees in the public street, and in the face of all, make avowal of my sin, and pray for pardon; and I called Elizabeth forward to me, and told her to tell one of the men to get off his horse and hold mine, that I might dismount, as I wished to pray. She advised me not to do so, but to wait till we had arrived at the convent; but I would not be persuaded, but prepared to get down (many people looking at me the while, for my servants and horses caused much observation), when suddenly I heard the bells of the church, which was but a short distance off, calling to vespers, so I thought I would go on there instead. I then again urged on my horse, and many people followed me, shewing much curiosity, and looking in my face, of which I took no heed then, but which at another time would have displeased me greatly.

When we had arrived at the church porch my men came forward, and I descended from my horse. I told the men to remain outside for me, while I and Elizabeth entered the church together. I found also the crowd followed me, but of this I took no heed, so bent was I on arriving at the great altar, where they were already lighting the candles. Over the great altar stood a tall, fair statue of the Virgin, and to her especially I determined to pray.

Shortly afterwards the priests entered, and the service

began. I threw myself on my knees, and fixing my eyes on the statue of the Virgin, I prayed to her fervently for help and consolation, and to help me out of my great trouble. I acknowledged myself to be a wicked sinner, and that I had the night before been sore tempted by the Evil One, and that I had seen many of his fiends; but that this was done not willingly on my part, but by the instigation of Satan. I entered the accursed place without being aware of its character. I said that if I could again obtain my peace of mind, and the full certainty that my sin had been forgiven, that I would willingly devote the remainder of my life and fortune to the service of God and his Holy Church.

Although I had prayed earnestly, I received no answer till I spoke of devoting myself to the service of the Church, and then I felt somewhat more comforted, as if my case were not hopeless, and I determined to pray to the Virgin still more earnestly to accept my poor services. I again commenced my prayer. That I might do it the more fervently, I fixed my eyes upon the statue, but I felt that the gaze of many of the people present was on my face, and it somewhat withdrew my attention. To avoid this interruption without moving my head, I raised my hands and pressed them on my face, to hide it from those around me.

A marvellous change took place within me. Although my eyes were fast closed, although my hands pressed over them on my face, the figure of the Blessed Virgin was as perfectly seen by me as before. She stood there as clearly and positively defined; not a feature in her face, not a fold in her dress, had altered. Before I could realise the wonder I beheld as being in any way strange, I saw the blessed image, on my again offering myself to the service of the Church, slowly and with dignity raise her right arm and thrice give me the benediction. My prayer suddenly ceased from awe, and wonder at the moment filled my mind. Presently I dropped my hands to look around me, and note in what manner the rest regarded the wonderful manifestation of the acceptance of my prayer, when I found by their unmoved countenances it had been seen by none but myself. Even the holy priest at the altar had not been aware of it. I was now convinced the miracle had been performed solely on my behalf, and humbly, with my head bent to the ground, did I thank Heaven for having accepted my offering.

When the service was over I arose from my knees and proceeded to the church porch, where I found my men with the horses waiting for me. I was soon again placed on my palfrey, and Elizabeth on hers, and we proceeded straightway to the convent, still accompanied by many people, to none of whom I now paid any attention, so fully occupied was my mind with the miracle I had witnessed. I now ordered a man to ride forward and give the portress at the convent notice of my arrival. He obeyed me, and a few minutes afterwards I entered its walls.

I found my dear cousin, the Lady Edith Barogh, waiting to receive me. She embraced me tenderly and affectionately; indeed, so warm was the love she shewed me, that had she been my own dear mother it could not have been greater. I afterwards went with her to her private chamber, and there passed the remainder of the evening with her. She told me what arrangements she had made for my reception, and informed me that I might consider myself as a free guest rather than a boarder, so long as my liberty did not interfere with the rules of the house.

To her great surprise, I told her that it was my intention to remain permanently with her, and to become a nun of the order. After a moment's reflection she replied,—

"My dear daughter, I do not deny that such a determination on your part would give me great pleasure, but those who join us must do so on mature and cool reflection. It would be a scandal on our holy house to receive as a novice a lady in the first grief of her widowhood. No; remain with us for some weeks or months, and then, should you be willing again to speak of it, I shall be most happy to listen to you."

I told her that I had already coolly decided; that it was done upon mature reflection, and with good and sufficient cause; and that, furthermore, I had prayed to the Holy Virgin to aid me in the matter, and that I had received her decided and marked approbation for the course I had determined to adopt.

She paused for a moment, and regarded me with fixed attention. She then told me she would speak to me further on the subject on another occasion. She, moreover, said she could perceive I was much fatigued with my journey, and advised me to take some refreshment and then go to my bed. This I opposed, saying that I was not hungry, nor was I so fatigued that I required rest; but she said smilingly that she was lady and mistress of all within these walls, and implicit obedience was one of its principal rules.

I made no further objection, and in a short time our supper was brought in by a lay sister. Although I had eaten nothing all day, although I wished to shew my obedience to the Abbess in all things, however small, I could not eat. When she perceived this she no longer pressed me, but told a lay sister to lead me to a room which had been prepared for me apart from the cells of the sisterhood, at which I was much grieved, as I now wished to live exactly according to the rules of the convent; but I resolved to be obedient in all things, and I made no objection.

I could obtain no rest that night. Early the next morning the Lady Abbess visited me, and finding me ill at ease, she sent the sister who had charge of the infirmary to see me. She, when she came, told me I was feverish, and must keep my bed. She further sent me some slight decoctions, which she said would calm me, and she bathed my bruised face and hands with warm water, and then left me, saying she would see me again in the afternoon. She was an aged woman, with a sweet, benevolent expression of countenance; but I missed the grave look of intelligence and wisdom which the priest at the castle wore when attending the sick, and I feared that the art of curing was not well understood at the convent. Nevertheless, it is but just to say her applications and decoctions did me great good. I slept well that night, and rose almost in health, though somewhat weakly, the next morning.

After breakfast I waited on my dear cousin, the Lady Abbess. She received me as kindly as before, and told me how much pleased she was to see me so much better, for she had feared on the night of my arrival that I should have a severe fit of illness, I looked so disturbed. She shortly afterwards walked with me in the garden of the convent, and she conversed with me for a long time about my dear lord, and the manner of his death, and many other things which it would be useless now for me to repeat. I answered her in all things truly and honestly; but I did not mention to her the miracle of the dead hand, nor the kind manifestation of the Virgin's acceptance of the offer of the remainder of my life in the service of God and the Church, as I had determined to confess to the confessor of the convent as soon as might be convenient, and I would then take his advice on all these subjects.

In the afternoon my cousin conducted me over the convent, and shewed me all parts of it,—the chapel, the cloister, the refectory, the infirmary, and even the kitchen. There she pointed out to me two of the sisters who were obliged to help the cooks and clean out the platters, as a punishment for using intemperate and harsh language to some of the children whom they had to instruct, as mildness and kind treatment to those in infancy, or the old and infirm, were among the strictest rules of the convent. The two sisters looked much ashamed of their punishment, and tears came into their eyes. I turned my head from them, not to cause them unnecessary pain; but at the same time I thanked God that I had entered a house where kindness and mercy were practised both to young and old.

In the evening I told my cousin I should like to confess whenever it was convenient, and she told me it could be when I pleased, so I asked her if I could do so on the morrow? She replied that I could; and immediately sent a lay sister to the reverend confessor (it was the holy father Robert, long since dead, but whom some of the elder sisters may still remember) to tell him to be in his confessional in the convent chapel at an hour before noon on the morrow.

The next morning I fasted till the appointed time, occupying my mind the while with prayer. When I knelt before the priest at the confessional, I was determined that not a fault should escape me that I could possibly remember. I first related what had been on my conscience before I left the castle, and my rebellious thoughts against the orders of the good priest on my way to the village at which I rested. I then described to him as well as I was able the terrible scene in the accursed circle of stones; how my mind was occupied first in finding false excuses to shorten the sojourn in the convent I had promised to make; secondly, my wishes again to mix in the vanities of the world; and lastly, my wickedness in wishing again for the friendship of the Vidame, whose acquaintance had already caused me so much misery. I then described to him the terrible scene which followed; how I had seen the fiends watching me with anxious countenances; my neglect in leaving my rosary at home when I had vowed it should never leave my side; and the terrible distress of mind I had suffered at the loss of my kerchief, fearing that I had unwillingly left it in the possession of the evil spirits that were around me at the time. I further told the reverend father of my great anxiety of mind during my journey to Wilton, and the miracle performed by the blessed Virgin in the church, and my resolution and vow thereupon to enter holy orders.

The reverend father listened with great patience and attention to my recital. When I had finished, he questioned me closely on all I had stated, and I honestly and openly answered every question he asked.

He told me I had sinned greatly at murmuring at the advice given me by the holy priest of St Botolph. He blamed my neglect of my rosary, when I so well knew its merits. To that neglect he traced my rebellious mind; and the attraction the circle of stones had had on me, he attributed also to my culpable carelessness in leaving it at home; for had I worn it, I had not been drawn with so much facility within the horrible magic circle,—a place notoriously formed for the worship of false gods, and now inhabited by fiends, as was well known to all the country round. My escape, he said, was most fortunate, and a proof of the goodness of Heaven towards me, for which I ought always to offer up praises and thanksgivings. He did not attribute the loss of the kerchief to the power of the fiends, and told me I had no reason to fear any unhappy result from that accident, which might easily have occurred elsewhere; but if I found the feeling of anxiety to continue, he would advise me to pray to be relieved from it, and if I did so with a fervent heart, he was certain my prayer would be accorded.

He dwelt at great length on the miracle in the church, and tried to shew me there was a possibility that I might have been mistaken; but I was too certain of it, and saw it far too clearly and positively to have been in error, and I would not (as, in truth to God, I ought not) admit that I had deceived myself. Finding that I had made no mistake, he next spoke about my taking the veil, as I wished. He said that of course I must pass the year of novitiate before taking the vows; but even to entertain the question, ought not to be done without grave consideration. In the frame of mind I was in when I first made the resolution, he should oppose my carrying out the intention, although the desire might be a most holy and laudable one. But the holy Church had many enemies, and no cause for scandal must be given. It must not be said that advantage was taken of a widow, in the grief of her widowhood, to induce her to enter holy orders, and bestow her wealth on her convent. He would advise me to remain some weeks before I was fully resolved, for then the sacrifice would be more acceptable, as my mind would be less biassed. In the meantime, I should pray for advice, and, if I resolved to carry out my present wish, that I might have fortitude to go through with it. He then ordered me certain penances, and my confession shortly afterwards concluded.

After I had left the confessional, my mind was in a far happier state than it had been for some time. I still resolved to become one of the sisterhood; at the same time, I admitted all the holy father had said to be just. With regard to the kerchief, my mind was also far more at ease than it was; but still not perfectly so: but I resolved to pray, as he had proposed, that it might be found, or that my mind might be easier. My penance I resolved to submit to patiently, and in every way to comport myself as a fitting candidate for the sisterhood.

For the next fortnight, nothing occurred worthy of especial notice. I submitted with patience and resignation to my penance, and conformed in all things to the strictest rules of the convent. Although these were not comprised in the penance the confessor had set me, I followed them that I might accustom myself to the severities of conventual life. Although with liberty to go outside the walls of the convent, I did not use it, with the exception of visiting some of the shrines in Salisbury Cathedral to offer up the prayers I had promised divers of my servants I would say for them. I did this the more scrupulously, as I should never see them again—the only sorrow I felt at the idea of entering the sisterhood, for I really loved my servants. They had shewed me so much respectful affection on the occasion of my lord's death, that it would have been wicked in me to have forgotten them. I can, however, conscientiously say they were always dear to me, and that, after having taken the vows, on all fitting occasions I inquired after them separately, and by name, and was always well pleased to hear they were happy.

One morning, when about a month of my sojourn in the convent had passed over, I was informed an aged priest wished to speak to me in the parlour. I immediately sought the discreet sister whose duty it was to be present at all interviews between the sisterhood and their friends, and went to meet him. To my great surprise, I found it was the old priest of the village where I had remained the memorable night that had caused me so much sin and misery.

He told me, with pleasure beaming on his face, that he had, through Heaven, been the means of finding the kerchief I had lost, and he had come to restore it to me. I cannot describe the great pleasure his intelligence gave me. Although on every other subject my mind was far happier since I had entered the convent than before, still the fact of the missing kerchief continued a source of incessant anxiety to me. I did not doubt the truth of my confessor's reasoning, but still I could not entirely divest my mind of the terror that night had caused me, even when aided by my prayers. Now all was set at rest by the kerchief being again in my possession.

When the priest offered it it to me, I hesitated a moment before I took it in my hand; but, being ashamed of my cowardice, I crossed myself, and received it from him; but immediately afterwards I placed it on a stool beside me. I then asked the old priest to explain to me the way it had come into his possession, although at the same time I felt some anxiety about his answer. But I had no cause for it. He told me he was not allowed to inform me of the particulars respecting its restoration, as it was a secret of the confessional. Sufficient to say, he received it from a person who had obtained it in such a manner as he thought did not entitle him to the reward I had offered, and that he had brought me back the gold ring I had left with him. He then offered me the ring, but I refused to receive it, and begged he would keep it in remembrance of me and my gratitude for all the trouble he had taken on my account in the matter. This, however, he refused to do, saying he had only done his duty; and, moreover, if he should keep the ring, the envious might say he had refused to give it to those who had found the kerchief, but was willing enough to keep it himself.

Seeing he did not speak without reason, I did not press him longer to keep the ring, but in its stead I gave him a rich and curiously painted missal, which I had brought with me, and which had been beautifully painted by expert artists in Italy. Also I made him take some money for the use of his poor, and beyond that, gave him in gold, for the purchase of new vestments for him to wear when celebrating the holy mass, twice the value of the ring he had returned to me. He thanked me many times for my generosity, although I would willingly not have heard him, for it went against my conscience to hear so good and aged a man thanking me so warmly for that which, after all, cost me so little, when the amount of my wealth was taken into consideration. He shortly afterwards left me, well content with his visit.

As soon as he had gone, I took up the kerchief from the stool on which I had thrown it. I did not grasp it in my hand as I should have done on ordinary occasions, but held it with the tips of my fingers, as something loathsome to me, and in that manner I carried it to my private room, when I immediately threw it on the floor. I then called for my servant Elizabeth, who came to me shortly afterwards. I commanded her to light me a fire, as I wanted one directly. She looked astonished at the order, and asked me if I were not well as I wished for a fire on so warm a day; but I desired she would not converse with me on the subject, but do as she was asked. Without more objection she immediately brought in some wood, and in a short time it was in a blaze. When I saw there was no danger of the fire going out, I desired Elizabeth to leave the room; and having fastened the door, I took up the kerchief and threw it on the flames. As it burnt I felt a strange sensation of satisfaction come over me. Notwithstanding the assurance the confessor had given me that I had no reason to fear any ill from losing my kerchief in the manner I did, still an unaccountable fear that danger hung over me oppressed me greatly; and had I not destroyed it, I should always have feared some accident might have arisen from it. Now, as I saw it gradually being consumed by the flames, my confidence rose in proportion. I gazed at it to the end. When, at last, it lay a charred, blackened cinder, I watched the lines of fire which traversed it, and each last spark which clung to them, till, in the end, no more appeared. I then rose from the ground, on which I had been seated, and gratefully thanked Heaven that my last terror connected with that fearful night was now extinct.

I had now been some months in the convent, and I considered it was not too early to declare to my cousin, the lady abbess, my fixed determination to adopt the conventual life. I had now no reason for further delay. The terror I was under when first I entered the convent had now entirely vanished, consequently that in no way could bias my decision. I had now been a widow for more than twelve months, therefore it could not be said I had taken my resolution while labouring under the first grief of my widowhood; for now, although I still loved the memory of my dear lord as tenderly as I did the day of his death, I could argue coolly and reasonably on the subject of quitting the outer world. It was with the hope of being reunited to my dear lord in Paradise that mainly induced me to be so firm in my determination. Since I had been in the convent, I had made a point of offering up a prayer for the peace of his soul each time I took the rosary in my hand, and I believe that each prayer I uttered for him increased the respectful love I bore for his memory.

Again, it could not now be said that the severities of a conventual life were unknown to me. Since my residence in the convent, I had followed rigorously the rules adopted by the other nuns, and found them neither irksome nor severe; on the contrary, I was well used to them, and liked them. I had daily employed myself in teaching the children of the poor of Wilton, for we had a child's school in the convent, and the sister who had the superintendence of it said that I wanted neither patience nor ability for the task, and I believe the children themselves loved no one of the sisterhood employed in teaching them better than they loved me. I had also taken my turn in the infirmary, and perhaps was fonder of caring for the sick than of teaching the young.

Although the refusal of the abbess, as well as the confessor, to entertain my offer of entering myself as a novice when first I arrived at the convent, gave me at the time some grief, I now perceived I had done well by waiting, and they wisely in advising it. Had they accepted my offer at the moment, it might have been said they had influenced me, though perhaps indirectly, in the matter; but I could perceive they had acted towards me in all honour. Not only the abbess and the confessor had abstained from influencing me, but neither they nor any of the sisters of the convent had given me the slightest hint they wished me to join them, so that now they could offer no objection on the score that my determination was not the effect of my own free will.

When I made the proposition to the abbess, she listened to me with great attention and evident pleasure. As soon as I had concluded, she kissed me affectionately, and told me my determination caused her great joy. That she had long wished to receive me into the sisterhood, but that knowing I was a young widow, and, moreover, that I had great wealth, she would not incur the scandal which might have arisen had she advised me on the subject. She then told me that I should further pray to Heaven to give me some indication that I was fitted for the vocation, if the smallest doubt yet remained in my mind on the subject. I told her, that as far as that went, I would do so if she ordered it, but that I had already offered up many prayers on the subject, and that I was fully convinced I should never regret the step I was about to take. The lady abbess, when she heard this, said she would no longer propose any delay, and that preparations should be immediately made to receive me as a novice.

I will not occupy your time with a description of the ceremony, with which you are all well acquainted. Suffice it to say, that happy as I had felt before it, my happiness increased after it had ended, and the nearer my noviciate approached its termination, the more attractive did the idea of entering the sisterhood for life appear to me. As each day passed, I offered up a prayer of thanksgiving that I was nearer the end I so ardently desired.

As the time approached for my taking the veil, it was necessary for me to dispose of some of my wealth, as far as money and jewels were concerned, and such dispositions concerning my lord's estate as the law considered requisite. For the latter I wrote to my scrivener, and requested his attendance on me at the convent. He arrived shortly afterwards, and received my instructions, as far as I was able to give them, for the disposal of my property, which he promised to carry out to the best of his abilities, and in accordance with the law of the land. He did so in due time, honourably and faithfully, and I have always had reason to be content with the arrangements he made.

I next wrote to my steward at the castle, requesting he would wait on me, and if possible bring Bertha and her husband with him, as I much wished to see them both. All three, a week afterwards, arrived in Wilton, and repaired to certain lodgings I had taken for them in the town. The day after their arrival, I first sent for Bertha to attend me, and (as I had obtained permission from the lady abbess) I received her in my private cell. It was some moments before we could speak, we were both so much agitated. At last she began—

"Dear lady, I always told you if once you entered the walls of this convent, you would remain here, and I should never see you more."

To which I replied, "You silly girl, what should hinder you from seeing me? It is not so far from the castle to Wilton as it is from the castle to London. There is no reason why you should not visit me every year, and remain some time with me, and that should content you."

But Bertha said she had a husband who would not like her to be absent from him, even though she should be in a convent. Not that he was jealous of her, but that he was too fond of her willingly to lose her company. But I told her I thought I had provided means to secure his permission, and though thereat Bertha shook her head, I knew I was right.

(Before she arrived, I had determined in my own mind, that if he would allow Bertha to remain with me for one month each year, she willing, I would let him have his land without rent or payment of any kind for the term of his life; but if he would not, he should pay as heretofore.)

I then spoke to her of the disposal of my worldly goods, such as were not valuable for the service of the convent. Among other things, I told her (with great fear and trembling on my part, for I knew her vanity) that it was my intention to give her the greater part of my dresses. I then looked at her, expecting to see her eyes, as usual, beam with pleasure at the idea of wearing fine clothes; but I was mistaken, and did her an injustice. Her eyes, on the contrary, filled with tears, and she said in a trembling voice—

"Dear lady, you do me wrong when you think a gift of this kind will console me for your absence; for I know you think so. I know I am too fond of dress, and that is my folly; but to allow it to compensate me for your absence, who have been so condescending and good to me, would be an ungrateful sin on my part."

The dear girl's words gave me great happiness, and we began to talk of other things connected with the castle and bygone days, all of which were unconnected with the subject before us.

The next day, Bertha and her husband presented themselves, with the steward, in the parlour, and I conversed with them a long time, the discreet sister whom I have already mentioned being present the while. I first spoke to Bertha's husband. I told him I hoped he would allow his wife to make me a visit annually, and for some weeks, and to make such an arrangement agreeable both to him and to her, I had already obtained permission of the abbess to allow her to remain in the convent during her residence with me.

I saw his face fell when I mentioned the subject, and that he was evidently preparing some excuse in his mind, so that he might be able civilly to refuse my offer. I then turned to my steward, and asked him whether it would be legal for me to grant to Bertha's husband a lease of his farm during the whole term of his life, without the payment of any rent, or charges of any kind, as I wished in some way to compensate him for his kindness in allowing his wife to visit me each year. (This I said aloud, as I knew her husband to be as fond of money as Bertha naturally was of dress.)

The steward told me I had the power to grant such a lease, if I pleased, upon the husband paying me some trifle each year, as a proof that I was still owner of the land, and that the tenant acknowledged my right. For example, it might be a rose at midsummer, or a fat capon at Christmas, or any other symbol of the sort.

I then turned to Bertha and her husband, who had been talking earnestly apart, she evidently trying to persuade him to allow her visit, and he finding some excuse for refusing her. But now his countenance had totally changed, and he seemed highly pleased, at the same time making great pretence that he had not heard my conversation with the steward; and when I related to him what I had resolved on, he appeared greatly pleased and surprised, and said it was too much goodness on my part to the like of him, and many other compliments of the kind, which signified nothing to me. At the same time he told me, what pleased me exceedingly, that he would willingly allow his wife to visit me for some weeks annually, as I proposed, being certain her residence in the convent, under my protection, would benefit her both in body and soul. Bertha made no remark on the arrangement, but I easily saw it pleased her greatly.

In a short time, Bertha and her husband left me, and I remained alone with my steward and the sister. I occupied myself for some time with the former, arranging the affairs of the castle and the estate surrounding it, all of which has no relation to this my confession. At last, I inquired of him in what condition was the fallen noble tree.

(I had already asked many questions respecting it of Bertha, all of which she had answered to the best of her ability, but not in a manner sufficiently satisfactory to me. Indeed, she did not know how greatly I was interested in it, as I had abstained from talking to her about it, knowing she was timorous and superstitious, and I did not wish to excite her fears.)

My steward told me he had taken great care of the tree, as I had desired. He had removed round it all the brushwood and weeds, so that it would decay but slowly. He had also cut many of the branches from the surrounding trees, so that it might appear as if it were intended to be taken care of. He had, further, given strict orders to the peasantry not in any way to meddle with it, although he was not obeyed so satisfactorily as he could wish. They seemed to think that, if the tree were neglected, they were justified in using its branches for fuel, and did not believe him when he told them it was my order they should not meddle with it.

This intelligence grieved me sorely; and I made with my steward certain arrangements for its better custody in future. I put apart certain funds to build two cottages near the spot, to each of which I gave an acre of garden-ground, and a certain portion of meal annually, and the pasture for a cow on the great meadows. Two peasants of godly life and conversation, with their wives, were to be chosen, who should reside in these cottages without payment, on condition that they, from time to time, cleared the ground around the fallen tree from weeds, and also prevent any people from cutting its branches for firewood, or any other excuse. I gave my steward, as a reason for these orders, that my life had been miraculously saved from the falling of the tree upon me, and for that reason I wished to shew my gratitude to Heaven for sparing me. After transacting other business with me, he took his leave.

As the time now rapidly approached for my taking the veil, I inquired of the lady abbess what preparations I should make for the ceremony. She informed me, she thought it should be conducted in a manner worthy of the high reputation of their house, the more so as the chapel of the convent would then be under repair, and it would be necessary that the ceremony of my admission should be performed in the great church in the town of Wilton, and that many people would be present.

I told her I was perfectly willing that it should take place in our chapel, though under repair, if she thought it advisable, as I wished to behave in all things with humility, but that of course I would be guided by her. She said I should consider the ceremony was not for my own glorification, but for that of religion, and that it was my duty that it should take place as magnificently as possible.

I bowed with willing respect to her opinion, and we then conversed about the dress I should wear on the occasion of my marriage with my Heavenly Bridegroom, in which she took great interest, and counselled me with such judgment that I marvelled at her great taste in the matter, and complimented her upon it, at which at first she laughed good-humouredly; but afterwards she said seriously that she only occupied herself about such matters when they were, as in the present instance, connected with the ceremonies of the Church.

(And I should not have mentioned the subject of my dress in this my confession, having long since lost all taste for vanities of the kind, but simply as shewing how great my wish was to render all proper respect to the ceremony of my admission into the sisterhood.)

A few days later, the lady abbess called me to her again, and asked what steps I intended to take about my dress? I informed her I was on the point of writing to London to the wife of my scrivener to find out among the tailors of London the one who could best make a rich wedding dress; but the abbess said I could do much better than that. She had a cousin who was abbess in a convent of Ursilines in Paris, and she was acquainted with all the noblest dames at the court. If I wished it, she would write to her cousin to inform me who among the tailors in Paris was then the most celebrated, and also to send me his advice in what way and of what stuff my robe should be made. To all this I gratefully assented, and she then desired me to leave her, that she might prepare her letter the more thoughtfully. In a few days afterwards, I asked the lady abbess' permission to allow Bertha to reside with me in the convent till the day I should take the veil, to which she willingly acceded.

Bertha arrived at the convent the day before the return of the messenger from Paris. After the man had given the letter into the hands of the abbess, I was called to her to hear it read. But I was not alone; for not only did Bertha accompany me, but many of the nuns, stimulated by a curiosity they could not restrain, hurried unbidden into the presence of the abbess. For this breach of the rules, as well as good manners, she rebuked them sharply, but noticing the expression of anxiety on their faces, she kindly allowed them to remain.

The letter was not very explanatory. The lady abbess of the Ursilines said that many and great changes had lately taken place in Paris in the wedding dresses of the brides of the court, but that the favourite stuff used at the present time was green velvet. Upon hearing this, Bertha said (foolishly) that I should look lovely in green velvet; but for this I rebuked her, and bade her hold her peace. The letter, however, concluded by an offer from the abbess of the Ursilines to purchase the velvet for me, and all other things which could best be obtained in Paris, should I wish it, and she would then send them by an experienced tailor to England, who would instruct me in what manner they should be worn.

This advice I immediately adopted, and the messenger was ordered directly to return to Paris with another letter, at which he sorely grumbled, and wickedly said he would rather be servant to the D—— than to a parcel of nuns. For this he was soundly rebuked by the abbess, who threatened him with severe punishment for his sinfulness; but, as there was no other messenger at hand, I thought it would be better to forgive him after admonishing him. Moreover, I promised a double payment if he travelled diligently, and this put him again in good humour, so all terminated pleasantly.

Three weeks later, and a fortnight before the ceremony was to take place, the messenger returned with the goods, and a French tailor. When the package was opened, it was edifying to see the interest the good nuns took, that the ceremony should be conducted with proper pomp and magnificence. So much did they handle the velvet and lace, that Bertha, in whose charge the dress was to be placed, was obliged to remonstrate with them, and tell them they would be injuring it if they were not more discreet. After every thing was arranged, and such regulations made that the tailor could go on with his work without scandal to the convent, we separated.

All went on smoothly for the next fortnight, when an obstacle for a moment presented itself. The Bishop of Salisbury sent to the abbess, and told her that, the Benedictines being a secluded order, the ceremony ought not to take place outside the convent walls; but upon a little remonstrance on the part of the lady abbess he withdrew his objection, and the day was fixed for the celebration.

In the mean time all was bustle within the convent walls, in making preparations for the eventful day. But perhaps the greatest interest of all was felt in the progress of the wedding dress; and from all grades of the nuns, from the lady abbess down to the humblest lay sister employed in the kitchen. To these last especially, the sight of the rich dresses was a great treat, and much did they thank me for my consideration in shewing them the various articles as they were in turn completed. But of all persons within the walls, the happiest perhaps was Bertha. She had now got over a great part of the sorrow she had formerly felt at the idea of my remaining for life within the convent walls, in consequence of the permission her husband had given her to visit me yearly, and she entered into the arrangement and formation of my dress with great ardour. At last all was in readiness, but only on the day before the ceremony was to take place.

On the morning of the day appointed for my taking the veil, I arose early, and humbly prepared myself by prayer for the coming ceremony. That over, I broke my fast, though this was done somewhat against my own inclination, on the advice of the lady abbess, who, fearing I might not have strength to go through the ceremony if I fasted, requested I would take some food before leaving the convent for the church.

After breakfast I called Bertha, and commenced arranging myself in my bridal dress. This occupied me nearly two hours, for I took great care that everything should be well and carefully arranged; and I not only succeeded to my own satisfaction, but to that of Bertha as well, who was greatly delighted with the appearance I made.

"Dear lady," she said, "how beautiful you look! It is not often that Heaven hath so handsome a bride."

But I immediately rebuked her for her impiety, though not harshly, for I remembered she was ignorant, and meant no harm; and more than that, her love for me had outweighed her discretion.

We now descended into the refectory, where the sisters were assembled to see me. When I entered the room a murmur of satisfaction arose from them all. The lady abbess advanced before the others, and said—

"My dear daughter, this day is one both of pleasure and satisfaction to me. Not on my own account solely, that I shall have always near me one I love so well, but that it is indeed a glory to our house, and a precious sacrifice to our holy Church, to receive one among us so well adapted to the respect and admiration of the outer world."

She then kissed me, and afterwards the sisters came round me and greatly admired my dress, asking me many questions respecting it. Although I have lost all love for such vanities, I will describe it, not that I take credit to myself for wearing it, but to shew my willingness to make as great a sacrifice of worldly adornment as I could when I entered into holy orders.

I wore no surcoat. The tailor sent by the French abbess of the Ursilines said that it was no longer worn in Paris. For this I was somewhat sorry, as I used to think it a most graceful garment. My robe, as I before said, was of green velvet. It was open to the waist, to shew a rich stomacher of lace, which was thickly studded with large pearls of great price. From the back, over my shoulders, and down to the buckle of my girdle, the turnover of my robe was of ermine fur; around my waist was a girdle of thick gold embroidery, fastened by a massive buckle of virgin gold, on which was cut the crest of my dear lord. From my girdle hung the rosary which had been blessed by the Holy Father at Rome, and which now never left me night nor day. I wore no train, that having become old-fashioned; but round the bottom of my robe, which reached to my feet, was a broad band of ermine, similar to the turnover round my neck. My shoes also were of velvet and embroidered gold. On my head I did not wear the high cap which had so long been in fashion, but a very low one instead, turning back from my forehead, behind my head; and to hold my hair was a net of gold-thread strung with pearls; and from the sides of my cap, behind my ears, were two small wings of gauze, spangled with gold.

The time had now arrived for me to enter the litter, and proceed to the church. When I had arrived there, I remained for some time in the vestry, waiting the arrival of the Bishop of Salisbury, who was to celebrate the mass. Before he came, I marked the hum of many voices in the church, and the movement of feet, which told me the building was crowded, and I requested Bertha, who was with me, to see if it were not so. She almost immediately returned, saying the building was so full, it would be difficult for another person to enter it. This made me feel for a moment afraid, but the feeling soon vanished when I remembered the duty I had to perform. Shortly afterwards the Bishop arrived, and the ceremony began.

I will not describe it to you; you have seen it too often not to understand it well. The church, as Bertha said, was crowded, but all remained quiet and attentive, and all passed off in a solemn and devout manner. When it was concluded, I remained a few moments longer on my knees before the altar. It was to offer up one short mental heartfelt prayer.

I prayed that for the sin and folly I had been guilty of in

shewing so much disrespect to my noble lord and dear husband, Heaven would be pleased to pardon me; and for the end that I might again be permitted to meet my dear husband in Paradise, I willingly renounced my youth, my wealth, and the world, and gave up my whole life to the service of God and His Church, in the strong hope my sacrifice might be found acceptable, and my petition favourably heard.

I then rose from my knees, and prepared to leave the church; but before doing so, I cast, for the first time, my eyes on the multitude of faces in it. But of all present, my eyes were fixed only on one. Before me, and close to me, dressed in all the magnificence of a noble, stood the Vidame. He bent his eyes fully on me, and I calmly received his gaze; nay more, I returned it, for the determination came over me to know what effect his presence now had on me, and I was well satisfied with the result. An indifference so perfect, an apathy so profound was over me at the moment, that had he been a peasant, or a carved image of wood, he could not have been less interesting to me. I continued my gaze for a moment longer, without the slightest variation in my feeling, and I then turned to enter the sacristy, where I should put off my bride's dress, and assume that of the convent, which I should never more quit. As I moved forward, an invisible hand took mine: but oh, how blessed was the sensation I now felt! It now seemed the hand of a loving mother conducting me to my spiritual Bridegroom; nor did it quit me till I had entered the sacristy.

Here ends the written confession of Alicia Longspee, ten years Lady Abbess of the Benedictine Convent at Wilton.

BY THE SAME AUTHOR.

One Vol., crown 8vo, cloth, price 6s.,

SHIRLEY HALL ASYLUM.

OPINIONS OF THE PRESS.

"The discovery of a modern story, where some attempt has been made to study truthfulness and nature, is a surprise as great as Crusoe's footprint in the sand. . . . . We may safely commend 'Shirley Hall Asylum' as a book far above the average of its kind. The originality, dry, Froissart-like humour, and versatile genius of its author, encourages us to expect hereafter something of a more sterling character from the same pen."—*The Times.*

"The writer's merits are very considerable indeed. The editor, who may be regarded as the real composer, has already published several other tales, one of these, entitled 'Margaret Meadows,' has been said to shew marks of a genius second only to that of Defoe. . . . . We can say, without hesitation, that the author, whether maniacal or not, knows how to tell a story, and tell it for the most part in capital unaffected English. The tales are all selected with a judgment and taste that go some way towards redeeming the book from close affinity with the ordinary sensation volume. . . . . A great deal of humour lightens the volume from beginning to end.—*Saturday Review.*

"The skill of the author is remarkably exhibited in the manner in which he has managed to delineate the aberrations of unsettled reason. . . . . Another success of the author is the constant presentation of insanity, without causing either repulsion or horror in the reader."—*Patriot.*

"This work possesses unquestionably both originality of conception and power of execution."—*Weekly Dispatch.*

"The tales treat necessarily of sufferings, but they are so remarkably well put together, that the sorrows of the leading character, instead of causing a painful feeling, create great interest. It is not often, among the shoals of new books that issue from the press, that we can so strongly recommend one for perusal as the present volume."—*Observer.*

"We would bespeak a hearty reception for this work; . . . but the whole volume is one of thrilling interest, and cannot fail to obtain deserved popularity."—*Dial.*

"As it is, we must ask our readers to accept our assurance that the book is thoroughly worth their attention; and they may take it up with the expectation of being entranced by its contents."—*Sunday Times.*

"This is a remarkable book, both on account of the nature of the subject, and the unusual merit of the execution; but even more so from the peculiarities of treatment, which isolate it from the mass of contemporary fiction."—*The Reader.*

"Supposing it not merely a 'tale founded on fact,' as the cant phrase is, but a veritable history, it would be one of the most remarkable productions in any language. It is pervaded by a spirit of strong vitality, and replete with passages of terrible interest."—*The British Standard.*

"The book is a powerful conception, replete with the higher qualifications of imagination."—*The Court Journal.*

"The stories are all extremely clever. The insanity illustrated by each is subtly mingled with the rational. . . . Most of the stories turn upon sad and painful incidents, but singularly enough the impression left upon the reader's mind is not painful."—*The Athenæum.*

"The author generally works, like De Foe, in copper, and frequently succeeds, like De Foe, in graving his notion on it so deeply and indelibly that it is even more striking than if it had had in it more of the transmuting touch of ordinary imaginative insight. Like De Foe, he almost always succeeds in making you think he is copying directly from actual experience, and not creating at all. . . . Yet there is more of distinct idea traced in these stories than De Foe ever admitted."—*The Spectator.*

"The author of Shirley Hall is already well known by a few works of remarkably graphic power—of power strong enough to enable him to write a book like that before us and leave people in the dark as to its foundation being authentic or imaginary. It might be either."—*Illustrated Times.*

"The subject is marvellously handled, and the author displays an acquaintance almost fearful with the peculiarities of the character he has assumed. . . . It is to no mere grave of the body that our author takes us; he descends into the charnel-house of the mind—he brings to our feasts of materialism in the nineteenth century the corpses of gigantic mental powers, and they tell us with one voice, as the Preacher told us thousands of years ago—*vanitas vanitatum.*"—*Tablet.*

"We have in the author of this remarkable volume a leader of thought in the department of fiction—a vigorous and truthful delineator of the varieties of human life—a profound and reverent student of those mysteries which are hidden from common eyes, and are alone decipherable in the hours of sorrow and darkness."—*Dumfriesshire Herald.*

"There is a singular skill in the management of all parts of this work—a marvellous consistency in the preservation of the precise mental condition assigned to the narrator. So skilfully is this managed, that the reader finds himself very often in doubt as to whether the biographer is not, after all, a perfectly sane man, who has really lighted on the track of some wonderful discovery. . . . Shirley Hall has now the rare merit of being thoroughly original and unique."—*Morning Star.*

"The case of Mainwaring is one in which the fixed idea has got a deeper and subtler hold of the mind than is ordinary, and is worth perusal, if only for the power with which the terrible scenes that occur between him and his mad wife are described."—*The Daily News.*

"There is a rare freshness and originality in these tales. We do not often meet with fiction so heartily and sincerely conceived. . . . The same merit—that of admirable unity of interest—distinguishes some of the other tales of Shirley Hall. The "Story of a Clergyman" is one which turns wholly on the downfall of an unhappy gentleman, who, in an evil hour, when overwhelmed with grief at the death of his only son, takes to drinking, and after long struggles to shake off that fatal habit, becomes the victim of *delirium tremens*, which finishes his career."—*The London Review.*

"Some of these memoirs are terrible,—such, for example, as 'Mainwaring's Confession,' and the 'Story of a Clergyman,'—and some of them are melancholy; and there are not a few ludicrous incidents at which gravity gives way, notwithstanding the sad fact that insanity in some of its many forms is before you."—*The Christian World.*

"Nervous readers may not be afraid of this volume though we tell them it is filled with the stories of ten lunatics."—*Weedon's Register of Facts.*

"The author of this remarkable book is a studious physiologist, as well as an original ethical philosopher, and has overlooked no facts in this domain of pyschology which were likely to promote its projects for alleviating the affliction of those unfortunates whom he considered the most miserable of the human race—the insane. . . . Our readers will find this work full of original thoughts and highly entertaining, and the pyschologist will rise enlightened after its careful perusal."—*The Lancet.*

"It is refreshing at a time when lunacy has become the cat's-paw of the sensation writers of the present day to meet a novelist who has the boldness to study the disease from nature, and the power of adapting it to the uses of legitimate fiction. The work is written with a De Foe-like graphicness which is as attractive as it is novel in these days of spasmodic literature."—*Pyschological Journal.*

MARGARET MEADOWS:

A TALE FOR THE PHARISEES.

By the Author of "Dives and Lazarus."

Crown 8vo, cloth, 2s. 6d.

"Contains a tale of real heroism and sad calamity in humble life, and the incidents are narrated in plain, terse, and forcible language. .... Its aim and object are to assist in raising a kindlier feeling among all classes by a consideration of the truth that among the humblest classes of life are to be found instances of self-sacrificing devotion, of sterling probity, and successful industry, not to be found in any other class of the community."—*Morning Chronicle.*

THE WEAVER'S FAMILY.

By the Author of "Margaret Meadows."

Foolscap, cloth, 2s. 6d.

www.ingramcontent.com/pod-product-compliance
Lightning Source LLC
Chambersburg PA
CBHW030349170426
43202CB00010B/1302